OTHER TITLES OF INTEREST FROM ST. LUCIE PRESS

Continual Improvement in Government: Tools and Methods

Transformational Leadership in Government

Teams in Government: A Handbook for Team-Based Organizations

Quality Government: Designing, Developing, and Implementing TQM

Total Quality Service: Principles, Practices and Implementation

The New Leader: Bringing Creativity and Innovation to the Workplace

Organization Teams: Building Continuous Quality Improvement

Leadership by Encouragement

The Motivating Team Leader

For more information about these titles call, fax or write:

St. Lucie Press
2000 Corporate Blvd., N.W.
Boca Raton, FL 33431-9868

TEL (561) 994-0555 • (800) 272-7737
FAX (800) 374-3401
E-MAIL information@slpress.com
WEB SITE http://www.slpress.com

$S\overset{t}{L}$

Second Edition

HOW TO WIN YOUR **1**ST ELECTION

Susan Guber

S^t_L

St. Lucie Press
Boca Raton, Florida

Phone: (561) 994-0555
E-mail: information@slpress.com
Web site: http://www.slpress.com

S$_L^t$

Published by
St. Lucie Press
2000 Corporate Blvd., N.W.
Boca Raton, FL 33431-9868

Table of Contents

Introduction

There is no magic formula to winning an election. Each election is unique. The mood of the electorate, the press, the economy, the caliber of the candidate, and the opponents all play a significant role.

The inner resources of the candidate play a big part, too. How much time can the candidate commit? Is he or she well organized, a self-starter, a fund-raiser? These are questions that must be asked.

There are lessons one can derive from successful races, but there is no recipe for what works and what doesn't. You must be willing to try it all. The late Claude Pepper, senior member of Congress, told me when he was eighty-six years old, "Perhaps the most important element in a successful campaign is the willingness and the will to win, the desire to win being so strong in the candidate that he or she will exert tremendous effort and dedication to the victory. In order to do that, in general a candidate must be the kind of person dedicated to the kind of public service that he or she seeks."

Predicting the results of an election is somewhat like reading a crystal ball; if there were predictable answers, elections would not be the horse races they are. This measure of the unknown makes them a competition, a challenge, and a game. This book provides the essentials for a well-run campaign. If a candidate doesn't win after using them, then it won't be because he or she did not campaign well. Of course, I would be foolish to say that is not important, but the means to that end can furnish priceless lessons. You can gain a lot of experience, skill, and personal insight by running. Win or lose, you will acquire experiences you never had before, meet new people, get involved in new organizations, become aware of public affairs, and, in short, grow. Running for office was truly the best year of my life. Sometimes when I look back, I think that running for office is at times more exciting than being in office. I looked forward to every campaign with enthusiasm.

One of the reasons I decided to write this book is that I ran in a district that was held by a Republican, that had never elected a woman to anything, and that has so many professional people living in it that I was bound to get lots of opposition. Indeed, more lawyers and doctors live in my district than in any other district in the state! The point is that it is possible to win against these obstacles, as I did. The key is to work hard and keep to a plan.

Another reason why I wrote the book is for the female candidate. Few women over the age of fifty have corporate experience. The glass ceiling has kept many women from moving up in their jobs or community service, where they would have the opportunity to develop relationships with chamber of commerce members or power brokers. How does a woman who wants to run get started? My recipe is especially directed toward that woman.

Finally, I wrote the book because there is so little written on the subject, particularly for candidates with no knowledge of the mechanisms of elections. People would ask if I would help them with their campaigns. I found I was spending hours with candidates, so I decided to put it all in writing.

I devoted fourteen months to running for office, working twelve to sixteen hours a day. I listened to the advice of many people, but ultimately I had to make my own decisions about what activities to undertake. Once I made my decision, I followed through—from start to finish. Here, then, is how I won my first election.

Acknowledgments

S pecial thanks to Norma Burke, who edited the book, and to my husband, Michael Guber, who critiqued the content.

Thanks to members of the Florida political community for answering my questionnaire so that I could include anecdotal examples from their campaigns.

My sincere gratitude to Dr. Allen Morris, the historian of the Florida legislature, for allowing me to quote from his book, *How to Win in Politics* (Peninsular Publishing, 1949).

About the Author

S usan Guber served three terms in the Florida House of Representatives. Prior to her election, she chaired Dade County Common Cause, the Citizen's Coalition for Public Schools, and the Women's Political Caucus.

Ms. Guber grew up in Brookline, Massachusetts and received her B.A. degree from the University of Chicago. For the past thirty-two years, she has lived in Miami, Florida. She has been married for thirty-eight years and has two married daughters and a granddaughter.

Currently Susan Guber is a lobbyist, mainly dealing with healthcare issues. She serves on the Florida Commission on the Status of Women and the Dade Cultural Affairs Council. She was recently elected chair of the Dade Cultural Alliance.

1

Deciding to Run

There are many reasons why a person decides to run for office. Among them are serving the community, solving problems, participating in the decisions that affect many, learning about government, and being a leader. Most people who run will give you a lengthy dissertation on their formal reasons for entering a race. The personal reasons are somewhat harder to come by. The real reason a person wants to submit himself or herself to the pressure of a tough political race, and then be under the watchful, critical eye of the public, is not easy to discern. Former thirty-year Congressman Dante Fascell said, "There are just four things you've got to know going in, though; you'll never get rich; you're under a microscope; there's no privacy; and you'd better work with other people because you're not a dictator. The democratic system is neither efficient nor economical."

When I asked State Representative Suzanne Jacobs of Delray Beach about her first race, she said, "It was a year long, arduous, back-breaking, exhausting experience." Asked if it was worth it, she answered "positively." Some people back into the decision inadvertently, like school board member Michael Krop. After seeing a newspaper article about so many people picking up applications to run and so few actually going through with it, he became an example of one who decided not to run. Then, one night he went to a restaurant, and a friend who had also read the same article said he was disappointed in Krop's decision. He spent ten minutes encouraging Krop, who was still unconvinced until the man whipped out his wallet and wrote a check. With his first contribution, he finally decided to make a go of it and became a school board member and then chair of the fourth largest school system in the United States.

Madeleine Kunin, former governor of Vermont, writes in her autobiography, "The first time I ran for office...it was by mistake." A local newspaper reporter covered a meeting she was attending at which she talked about the importance of women serving in public life. The reporter stood up at the meeting and said, "It's time for a woman," and announced Kunin would be running. Since she did not withdraw, she says it was the only way that she could step over the threshold into public life.

Most great leaders of this country began their political careers by making the decision to run in just the same way you or I would. Barbara Jordan, the first black woman elected to Congress from the South and a notable member of the Judiciary Committee to study the impeachment of a president, gives us a glimpse into her decision. In the book *Barbara Jordan, A Self Portrait,* she talks about John Kennedy's presidential campaign. She went down to headquarters to see if she could offer her assistance and volunteered to do anything. After stuffing envelopes for days, she was asked to fill in for the candidate at a speaking engagement. The campaign staff realized her speaking ability was outstanding and continued to use her in the role for which she is now famous. She says, "By the time the Kennedy-Johnson campaign ended successfully, I had really been bitten by the political bug. My interest, which had been latent, was sparked." One day, a friend said she should run for the Texas House of Representatives. She said, "I make enough money to eat and buy my clothes and run my little Simca, but I certainly don't make enough money to run a political campaign." After the friend loaned her the filing fee, she thought, "I've got to get serious about this. I've been talking politics, and wanting to get into it, and here I am." She questioned her knowledge about Texas state government and got a textbook to read up on the subject. Thus began her illustrious career.

Not all famous politicians have a hidden desire to run. Dwight Eisenhower backed into running for president after stating repeatedly he had no desire for elected office. People asked him constantly if he would run for president. In his book *At Ease, Stories I Tell to Friends,* Eisenhower says, "Pressures increased. Finally, I took a convenient opportunity to put my views before the public in an answer I sent to a newspaper publisher who wanted to enter my name in the New Hampshire presidential primary of March 1948. I worked over the draft of the letter carefully because I did not want to make it appear that I was arrogant or aloof or not complimented by such suggestions as had been made—but I did want to make it definite that I was not going to get involved in politics." Not taking no for an answer, he was asked to speak along with other "candidates" at the Republican National Convention. He wrote a letter saying he was not a candidate but that "tremendous demands had developed urging me to get into politics. These came from both parties. Men of every kind and class, it seemed, visited my headquarters during all of 1951 and each had his own reason for asserting that I owed it to the country to become a political candidate....For weeks I had to wrestle with the facts and arguments so often and so long presented. Finally, I came to the conclusion that with numerous people I deeply respected stressing the need of our country for a change in political control and domestic programs, I should abide by the decisions of my party and of the electorate if I were nominated." Thus Eisenhower threw his hat into the presidential ring and won by a landslide.

Personally, when asked the question, I would answer, "I've always had a fascination with the government process, its power, and the people who are in a position to make things happen." My first political involvement was in Common Cause, an organization that scrutinized the workings of government. I learned how money was raised for candidates, how lobbyists influenced the process, and how congressional rules worked. It gave me the background on general issues and how to lobby effectively. I then got two jobs at which I stayed two years each, both of which broadened my political background. One was an aide to a county commissioner, and the other was an aide to a state representative. After that, I was in charge of the legislative coordination between the local hospital association and state government. By the time I had served in all of these positions, I felt it was time for me to stop working around the system and run for office myself.

As I talked to other elected officials, I found they had similar reasons for running. One man had served on his local zoning board when he decided to run for his first elected office, the state senate. Another had been president of his chamber of commerce, and still another had been a labor leader. George Crady, a member of the Florida House since 1977, lost twice before he won and sums up his first campaign as follows:

> There's gratitude for all of those who pleaded that I run.
>
> Convincing were the arguments campaigning would be fun.
>
> Announcement day was really swell, this said without retort,

Three hundred fifty relatives showed up to give support.

The campaign posters came at last two thousand forty-four,

Within three days they were gone and friends demanded more.

The day I stood there waiving signs, what glory did I see?

My bumper stickers totaled four hundred eighty three.

And thirteen thousand hands I shook while knocking door-to-door.

Behind each hand, a smiling face would pledge support galore.

Twelve thousand votes—the minimum—would be the count for me.

(Alas) the race was lost. I now admit a recount was not due.

But those who showed to vote for me my thanks, TO BOTH OF YOU!

Representative Crady had a sense of humor about his losses and decided to run a third time. Almost everyone who runs for election has been involved in some way in the community beforehand. They all have a bit of name recognition and a network of people to help them. Their reasons for running are as varied as the candidates themselves, and *why* becomes a frequently asked question on the campaign trail. Be prepared to sit down and think about why you want the office you are seeking and come up with some personal answers.

■ **Before you start campaigning, know your reasons for deciding to run and be able to articulate them. People will ask!**

2

Getting Involved

Some people are lucky enough to begin their quest for office with built-in name recognition. Either they were born with a famous name or a family member became well known after they were born. Having lots of money can be a big help, too.

Nelson Rockefeller, former governor of New York, had a world-famous grandfather who was the founder of Standard Oil. John F. Kennedy's father, Joe, was head of the Securities and Exchange Commission under President Roosevelt. Kennedy's maternal grandfather was the mayor of Boston. Such ties obviously give a person a huge edge. An election seems to be theirs to lose, because they start out so well known and financed. I can't help thinking that a name like Ford in Michigan helped Gerald Ford when he first ran for Congress, even though he is no relation to the automotive family.

Then there are those who have a well-known name from a previous profession. Ronald Reagan was a famous actor before he ran for governor of California, and Dwight Eisenhower was a World War II general and hero.

Some people have family members who pave the way. Susan Molinary, a congresswoman from New York, had a grandfather who was a fixture in Staten Island politics and a father who gave up his congressional seat to run for Staten Island borough president. Representative Molinary then ran for her father's House seat.

Olympia Snowe,[1] congresswoman from Maine, was married to the governor of Maine. They do not have the same name, but having the governor as your spouse is a tremendous help.

Most people who decide to run have no ties to people in office other than what they create. Senator Barbara Mikulski[2] of Maryland was a citizen lobbyist in the sixties and fought to halt construction of a proposed highway through several established neighborhoods. She then ran for the Baltimore City Council and served five years. Representative Jane Harman from California got an incredible education at Smith College and Harvard Law School. She secured a job as aide to a U.S. senator and then to President Jimmy Carter. Her husband is founder of a large corporation. When it was time for her to run, she had money as well as fabulous credentials.

Getting a job as a legislative aide is easier than you may think. Many of the elected officials come up through the ranks as an aide first. Looking back at my legislative career, I never would have run for office without being an aide first. How would I have known I would like the job if I did not know what it entailed? It would be a shame to go through the trials of running a campaign to find out you hate the job, especially one that costs so much time and money to attain.

The easiest way to get hired as an aide is to work in the campaign of a person who is running. Frank Morra, my loyal legislative staff person, started with me in my home putting together a mailing. He came to my house several nights a week to help me with my daily canvassing. It was a natural for me to hire him as I had already worked with him for months. I began as a campaign worker as well, helping with door-to-door walks and with phone banks. I served as an aide to a county commissioner for two years and then as an aide to a state representative.

If it is not election time and you want to serve as an assistant, large counties have a central office for state legislators. Get the director of that office to put your name on a list of potential aides. Often, aides leave service, and the elected official has to find a new assistant quickly. Try to meet as many of the elected officials as possible. Then, when an opening arises, you can fill the job.

The most common way to begin seeking public office is to get involved in the community. Look into various organizations in your community, including:

- Chambers of commerce
- Churches and synagogues
- Political action groups (EMILY'S List, NOW, Builders Association, Bankers Clubs)
- Parent-Teacher Associations (PTAs)
- Service clubs (Rotary, Kiwanis, Civitan)

Pick out two or three groups that especially interest you and join them. (You can find out when and where they meet by looking in the neighborhood section of your local newspaper, watching the community calendar on TV, or listening to it on radio.) Become an active member and gain some visibility in your community.

Twenty years ago, I joined the Miami chapter of a national lobby group called Common Cause. At my first meeting, I was asked to be program chairperson. I had no idea what a program chair did, but it was an opportunity to learn. It turned out to be a great experience. By having interesting meetings, I generated a good turnout and had the opportunity to meet many people who were involved and interested in government. These people were from the county, the state, the federal government, and the press. I became known as the Common Cause voice in my county. A few years later, I was elected president of the organization and a member of the state governing board.

These positions gave me visibility and a bit of authority. When the press had a question on one of the issues our organization championed, they called me. Also, I wrote letters to the editor at the leading newspapers. In seven years of working as a volunteer for Common Cause, I had twenty-eight letters published, which was great for name recognition!

Each organization you join has its unique set of benefits. Here's a list of some of the other organizations I joined and the ways they helped me in my campaign:

- *Hospital Guild*—This was a network of wives of physicians who volunteered to walk door to door and telephone voters during the campaign.

- *League of Women Voters*—The former presidents sent out a letter to voters on my behalf.

- *Chambers of Commerce*—I joined several chambers in my district. Members contributed money and gave me a network of people to call upon. They also provided mailing lists of retailers in their areas that I went after for money.

- *Tennis Club*—They raised money from house parties, put up my signs in their businesses, and spread the word about my campaign.

- *Toastmasters International*—This organization, dedicated to the art of public speaking, had chapters all over the district. I made sure I spoke at each chapter, and they in turn provided volunteers.

I did not have to be active in all the organizations that I joined. I belonged to some just to show that I believed in their cause, and by the same token, many wound up doing the same for me.

When I decided to run, I was already in my forties, and my children were in high school. My original interest in running came from my parents, who were fascinated with politics and discussed it at the dinner table each night. Had I thought about office for myself, I would have begun getting ready in school. Alas, I went to school in the fifties, when very few women even thought about anything other than being wives and mothers. Nevertheless, high schools, colleges, and universities are great training grounds for future politicians. Most campuses have a student government. My daughter Elizabeth won the Coral Gables Senior High School presidency in 1982 after giving campaign speeches in both English and Spanish. It was a gimmick she used based on a gut feeling that she would need the Hispanic vote to win. My other daughter, Carolyn, went dorm to dorm in her quest for a student senate seat at Tufts University. Student campaigns have all the elements of a real run for office in that candidates have to raise money, create publicity, and give speeches.

Most colleges have chapters of Young Democrats and Young Republicans. If those in your area don't, call your party headquarters and ask how to begin. State Representative Mike Abrams from Miami began his political career as president of the Young Democrats at the University of Miami; he went on to chair the Democratic Party in Dade County and then run for state office. He was so well known that he won his first race.

Finally, it helps if you have a cause and you become well known for it, as Senator Barbara Mikulski did. Whether it is as volatile as abortion or as passive as procurement of more park lands, speak out, become an authority, and make a good name for yourself. That is always a safe and traditional avenue to the political process.

- ■ Increase your political awareness and visibility by getting involved in community organizations such as charities, political clubs, chambers of commerce, PTAs, and special interest groups.

- ■ Take a direct and active role in community projects and events.

- ■ Gain access to the media by becoming a speaker for an organization.

References

1. Congressional Quarterly Politics in America, Congressional Quarterly Political Staff, Plil Duncan, Editor, 1994.
2. Women in Congress, U.S. House of Representatives, 1991.

3

Using the
Elections Department

Your elections department is a great resource, and the personnel who work there are your allies. The department is listed in the phone book under "elections" or "county government." These are the staff people who actually run the elections, but they are there to help candidates as well. Call the director of elections and make an appointment to meet him or her. In large counties, such as mine, there is a separate staff member for candidates. That woman was invaluable to me when I ran. Candidates may not always be easy to deal with, as they are highly visible while constantly under pressure. The elections department staff is prepared to deal with all the personalities and issues that they encounter, because they want elections to run smoothly for the candidates as well as the voters. If you start your campaign early, the elections staff will have more time for you, before they have many other candidates to deal with.

In addition to providing valuable counsel, the elections department sells an assortment of documents you will find indispensable in formulating your campaign strategy. Fourteen months before the election, I made my first trip to the department and purchased a map of my county. At the bottom of the map was a key to the voting precincts in the district in which I would be running. With a colored magic marker, I outlined all of my district. It was only then that I came to fully appreciate the size and scope of the area. The following weekend, my husband and I drove the periphery; I sat on the passenger side reading off the boundaries, while he drove. During that ride, I saw exactly what constituted the district: homes, businesses, farms, schools, churches, synagogues, and stretches of bay front. It also gave me a feeling for the types of people with whom I would be dealing. It took us more than two hours to travel the circumference, and I realized that my campaign was not going to be easy.

Another purchase I made at the elections department was a statistical breakdown of the groups of people who make up the district, known as the demographics. The breakdown listed the numbers of registered Republicans, Democrats, and Independents, along with the numbers of Anglos, Hispanics, First Americans, and Afro-Americans. In some counties, you can get a breakdown of Hispanics by country of origin. Puerto Ricans traditionally have registered Democratic, while Cubans have registered Republican. Age plays a factor in elections, as does gender. Women vote in greater percentages than men and will look for female candidates. White men between the ages of eighteen and thirty-five will vote for Republican men.

A third item that I bought was a history of past elections in the district. Unless the demographics have changed dramatically in the last two years, the results of past elections tell you what demographic groups vote in what numbers and in what type of election. In cities with large immigrant populations, the demographics can change rapidly, as they did in Miami. Incumbents who enjoyed landslide victories one year were has-beens two years later.

Some groups do not tend to vote in primaries or referendum elections. If you are running in a special election, this information should be taken into consideration. Most election data, however, give trends that carry over from one election to another.

The type of election is important. There are two types: primary and general. If other members of your party are competing for the office you seek, you will have to run against them in a primary election. Primary elections are for party members only. Democrats vote for Democrats, and Republicans vote for Republicans. The outcome yields the party's nominee to run in the general election against the other party's nominee.

In most Southern states, a second primary, or run-off, is held in the event none of the party's candidates receives a majority of the vote. In my race, there were six Democratic candidates. I won 42% of the vote in the first primary—not enough to win but enough to be in the run-off a month later. In that election, I received 62% of the vote, which enabled me to run in the November general election as my party's nominee. What is important is that the strategy that you employ in the general election will be different from the one you use in the primary, because you will have to reach a greater number of voters from both parties in the general election.

Some groups vote in high percentages compared with their actual numbers. These "activists" are often more influential in the outcome of an election than are voters from larger groups. For example, older and more affluent people vote in proportionately higher percentages. If your district has a large number of senior citizens, then the voter turnout will be high. If you are a Democrat and the seniors are Democrats, it's to your advantage to get them to the polls. If your district has a majority of senior citizens, then your campaign message had better appeal to senior citizens. If you are over sixty-five, then you have an added advantage, because the senior voters will identify with you. Be sure you tell people that you are a senior in your campaign literature.

Demographic information will give you an idea of what issues you will need to focus on and how the voters are likely to react to your candidacy. The more a candidate has in common with his or her constituency, the more likely he or she is to get their votes. If you are black and your district is 6% black and 80% Republican, then I'd advise you to look elsewhere to run. It may seem like common sense, but it is amazing how many people run in an area where they are personally out of sync. You don't need an expert to decide whether you are in tune with the district; just look at the numbers and make an educated calculation.

In planning your strategy, also consider whether it is a presidential election year. If it is, your candidacy may be favored by certain circumstances not present in off-year elections. Understand that more people will be voting, both in numbers and percentages. If the president is popular, then being a member of his party can help. In a presidential election year, there can be a "coattail" effect if a popular president is running for re-election. For example, Ronald Reagan was so popular in 1980 and 1984 that Republicans across the nation were virtually swept into office on the tide of his popularity. In an off-year election, a popular governor or senator can help a candidate. There is also a negative coattail effect if the person at the top is about to be dumped. A good example of that is when Jimmy Carter ran for re-election.

In presidential election years, media time is concentrated on the major candidates. Therefore, it will be more difficult for you to get free publicity, and you will have to depend upon mail, radio, or door-to-door canvassing.

Placement on the ballot also comes into play. If the office you are seeking appears at the top of the ballot, more people are likely to cast a vote for that office. Statistics show that candidates whose names appear farther down the list on the ballot receive fewer votes because voters often do not have the tenacity to vote the entire ballot. Races have been lost because a candidate failed to tell likely voters that his or her name appeared way down on the list. Within your race, placement of names is in alphabetical order, and voters will vote for the first name unless you tell them to look for your name farther down the list.

I won my first election during an off-year election. Because the office of the president was not on the ballot, I couldn't count on a large voter turnout. I had to get the voters out myself, which helped because I could target those voters who demographically were likely to vote for me.

They say that history repeats itself. Thus, by studying a district's past, you may gain insight into its future. Sometimes history is pretty recent. The district I ran in was created only four years prior to my election. In effect, I was running in a new area. In 1992, the laws by which lines are drawn were changed to create districts that had minority representation. The configuration of some new districts is so bizarre that the U.S. Supreme Court has determined that some may be illegally drawn.

Every decade, there is a national census. According to the population shift, lines are redrawn for political subdivisions. This process, known as redistricting, determines how the districts are actually drawn. By studying the demographics of an area, you will be are able to make an educated guess as to how the people in the district will vote.

Take full advantage of your elections department as you plan your campaign strategy. Make an appointment and meet with the staff. Find out what materials you can purchase to give you some insight into the race in which you will be running.

- **Get to know your local elections office personnel, and find out what resources the office can provide.**

- **Study the geographic composition of the area you intend to represent.**

- **Research the voting history of the area for an indication of your chances of receiving votes.**

- **Consider the type of election year in which you will be a candidate.**

- **If necessary, enlist the help of a political science expert at your local community college to assist in analyzing the implications of the information you collect. Then plan an effective election strategy.**

Note: Special thanks to Gisela Salas, assistant supervisor of elections for Metro-Dade County Department of Elections.

Items for sale

JANUARY 31, 1995

Items Available

1. Campaign Financing and Qualifying Packet (includes F.S. Chapter 106 for all candidates, and Chapters 99, 105 and 106 for judicial candidates) - Free
2. Election Law Book - $11.50/copy or on computer diskette - $5.00
3. GIS District and Street Maps - $5.00 each
4. Precinct Maps of Dade County
   - GIS Color $5.00
   - Black and White $2.00/set
5. Copies of the following are available at $.15 per page.*
   - Precinct-by Precinct voter registration statistics
   - Polling Places List
   - Campaign reports (Reports for Municipal candidates are available from respective City Clerks.)
   - Election results
   - Financial Disclosure Statements
   - List of Elected Officials
   - List of pollworkers on file by precincts. List of pollworkers assigned to work in an election by precinct is available approximately two weeks before an election.
   - Pollwatcher forms
6. Certifications - $1.00 each
7. Election results and book closing statistics on computer diskettes, available for elections since 9/3/91. Canvass Report Format (PRN files) - $5.00 each

* Two sided copies - $.20 per page
  No charge for up to 3 copies.

Magnetic Tapes

Magnetic Tapes are available for the following:

- Registered voters
- Voters who voted

At a cost of $.32 per 1000 names.

There is an additional $25.00 Service charge for each order.

- Voter History - flat fee of $340.00

Checks for voter history tapes must be made payable to (I.T.D) Information Technology Department.

Requirements for Obtaining Lists, Labels and Tapes

An Oath Form must be filed stating that lists, labels and tapes will be used solely for political purposes and not for commercial purposes.

Lists, labels and magnetic tapes are available only to the following:

☑ Candidates
☑ Incumbent Officeholders
☑ Political Parties (Rep., Dem., Minor Parties, etc.)
☑ Political Action Committees (Federal, State, County)
☑ Registered Committees of Continuous Existence
☑ Government Agencies
☑ Courts for jury selection

Candidates and incumbent officeholders can only purchase lists, labels or tapes of their respective district or municipality.

All orders will be paid in the following manner:

- All Candidates - Campaign Check
- Incumbents - Personal Check, Office Account Check
- Political Parties - Party Check
- Political Action Committees and Committees of Continuous Existence - Committee Check

Reference: Florida Statute 98.211

Lists and Labels

- Printed Lists - $3.50 per 1000 names
- Labels - $7.00 per 1000 names

There is an additional $15.00 Service Charge for each order placed.

Lists and Labels may be ordered in the following format:

- Registered Voters (Alpha, Street or Zipcode)
- Voters who Voted (Precinct, Party, Alpha only)
- Households (Precinct/Zipcode or Zipcode only)
- New Voters (Precinct/Alpha,Precinct/Zipcode or Zipcode only)
- Absentee Ballot mailing list for current calendar year (Precinct/Alpha,Precinct/Zipcode or Zipcode only)

Checks for all items unless otherwise noted must be made payable to the Board of County Commissioners.

For more information regarding items available for sale contact the Metro-Dade Elections Department, Public Services Division at 375-4382.

Metro-Dade Elections Department

Elections department resources

1996 Candidate Qualifying Information

STATE ELECTIONS   **April 1995**

Statewide Election Dates

First Primary	September 3, 1996
Second Primary	October 1, 1996
General Election	November 5, 1996

Who is a Candidate?

"Candidate" means any person to whom any one or more of the following apply:

a. Any person who seeks to qualify for nomination or election by means of the petitioning process.

b. Any person who seeks to qualify for election as a write-in candidate.

c. Any person who receives contributions or makes expenditures, or gives his consent for any other person to receive contributions or make expenditures, with a view to bring about his nomination or election to, or retention in, public office.

d. Any person who appoints a treasurer and designates a primary depository.

e. Any person who files qualification papers and subscribes to a candidate's oath as required by law.

However, this definition does not include any candidate for a political party executive committee.

Reference: Florida Statute 106.011 (16)

How to Begin Your Account

♦ Appoint your Campaign Treasurer.

1. The Treasurer must be a Florida registered voter.

2. The Candidate may be their own Treasurer or Deputy Treasurer.

3. Deputy Treasurers may be appointed when you open the account or at a later date.

♦ Open your Campaign Account at a bank authorized to do business in Florida.

1. The account must be separate from any personal or business account.

2. The bank will provide you with deposit slips and checks. Statements will be sent to the Campaign Treasurer.

♦ Complete the "Appointment of Campaign Treasurer and Designation of Campaign Depository" form.

1. Statewide and Legislative Candidates should return the original and one copy to:

Division of Elections
The Capitol, Room 1801, Tallahassee, FL 32301

An additional copy of all reports for other than statewide candidates must be filed with the Supervisor of Elections in the county where the candidate resides.

♦ Personal use of campaign funds by the candidate for salary or to defray normal living expenses is permitted only if you file a statement that you intend to do so. This statement must accompany the "Appointment of Campaign Treasurer and Designation of Campaign Depository for Candidate."

Reference: Florida Statute 106.023

♦ File the Statement of Candidate form within 10 days of filing the Appointment of Campaign Treasurer and Designation of Campaign Depository form, stating that the candidate has read and understands the requirements of Florida Statutes Chapter 106.

Reference: Florida Statute 106.023

When to Qualify

Statewide and Legislative candidates must qualify between:
Noon, July 15 to noon, July 19, 1996

Where to Qualify

All qualifying papers (One original and one copy) must be submitted to:

Division of Elections
The Capitol, Room 1801
Tallahassee, Florida 32301
(904) 488-7690

Elections department resources

What to File When Qualifying

1. "Appointment of Campaign Treasurer and Designation of Campaign Depository for Candidates" Form - if not already on file, (if applicable) "Statement of Intent" - If the candidate intends to use funds in the campaign to defray "normal living expenses" for themselves and their family, this statement must be filed at the same time as the "Appointment of Campaign Treasurer and Designation of Campaign Depository" form.
Reference : Florida Statute 106.1405

2. "Statement of Candidate" Form - if not already on file.

3. "Loyalty Oath/Oath of Candidate/Statement of Candidate" forms.

4. Financial Disclosure
"Form 6, Full and Public Disclosure of Financial Interests 1995"
*Reference:*Art. II, Sec. 8 (a) and (h), Florida Constitution and F.S. 112.3144).

5. Qualifying Fee - Must be paid by check drawn from campaign account. No personal checks will be accepted. Only candidates who withdraw prior to the end of qualifying will be refunded their qualifying fee. Anyone who withdraws after that time will not have their qualifying fee refunded.
Reference: Florida Statute: 99.092 (1)

If applicable: Resign to run - Must resign from elective or appointive office not less than 10 days prior to the first day of qualifying.
Reference: Florida Statute: 99.012

Name on the Ballot

A candidate's name will be printed on the ballot in the same form as it appears on the Candidate's Oath. A candidate may use a nickname indicated with " " or ( ). No titles will be printed on the ballot , i.e., Mr., Mrs., Ms., Dr., etc.
Reference: DE 86-06, AGO 051-343

Fund Raisers

The person for whom a campaign fund raiser is held must be a candidate. It is not necessary to file any forms showing intent to hold a fund raiser. Any tickets or advertisement must comply with the provisions listed in F.S. 106.025

Petty Cash

A candidate may withdraw $500 per quarter until qualifying ends. After qualifying ends, $100 may be withdrawn per week for candidates other than statewide seats.

Petty cash must be spent in amounts less than $30 and only for office supplies, transportation expenses and other necessities.
Reference: Florida Statute 106.12

Contributions

Limited to $500.00 per person per election.
Reference : Florida Statute 106.08

Contributions over $100.00 must list occupation.
Reference : Florida Statute 106.07

Cash contributions cannot exceed $100 per person.
Reference: Florida Statute 106.09

All contributions must be deposited in the campaign account prior to the 5th business day following its receipt.
Reference: Florida Statute 106.05

Any person making an in-kind contribution shall, at the time of making the contribution, place a value on the contribution. In-kind contributions are limited to $500 per election per person.
Reference: Florida Statute 106.055

The deadline for accepting contributions is 5 days prior to the day of the election (for Tuesday elections, the deadline is midnight the Thursday before the election.) Any contributions received after the deadline must be returned to the contributor.

Any contribution received by the candidate after the date which the candidate withdraws, is defeated, elected or becomes unopposed, shall be returned to the person contributing it and shall not be used or expended by the candidate.
Reference : Florida Statute 106.08(3)

If the candidate changes the designated office for which he is a candidate, he must notify all contributors in writing of his intent to seek a different office and offer to return pro rata, upon their request those contributions given in support of the original office sought. This notification shall be given within 15 days after the filing of the change of designation and shall include a standard form developed by the Division of Elections [DS-DE-2 (9-91)] for requesting the return of the contribution.
Reference : Florida Statute 106.021(1)(a)

Elections department resources

Expenditures

All expenditures, other than petty cash, must be made by a check drawn on the campaign account.

There must be enough money on deposit to cover the expenditure at the time of the payment.

Reference : Florida Statute 106.11(3)

Independent Expenditures

An independent expenditure is one which is not controlled by, coordinated with or made upon consultation with a candidate or political committee, or agent of a candidate or political committee. Any person spending $100 or more for a candidate or issue must file reports of such expenditures with the filing officer in the same manner and at the same time as a political committee. No one may make more than a $1,000 contribution to another person to be used as an independent expenditure.

Reference: Florida Statute 106.071

Independent Expenditure Disclaimer

An independent political advertisement must have the following disclaimer: "paid political advertisement paid for by (Name of person or committee paying for advertisement) independently of any candidate or committee."

Statement of Endorsement or Opposition

Any group, except those affiliated with political parties which endorses or opposes a candidate or issue by political advertisement, must file certain information with the filing officer. If the group endorses a candidate, the political advertisement must state whether the permission of the candidate has been obtained to advertise the endorsement. The information filed with the filing officer includes: date group formed, number of members, dues, officers, how endorsement or opposition to candidate or issue was decided, source of funds for political advertisement if not from dues and amount of funds paid to group by candidate.

Reference: Florida Statute 106.143(2) & 106.144

What is a political advertisement?

A political advertisement is a paid expression in any communication media which supports or opposes a candidate, elected public official or issue. Newsletters of organizations established prior to qualifying or issue being placed on the ballot are exempt if sent only to members.

Reference : Florida Statute 106.11(3)

No political advertisement of a candidate who is not an incumbent of the office for which he is running shall use the word "re-elect." Additionally, such advertisement must include the word "for" between the candidate's name and the office for which he is running.

Reference : Florida Statute 106.143(4)

Political Advertisement Disclaimer

All political advertisements must contain the following information:

1. "Paid political advertisement" or "pd. pol. adv."
2. The identity of the person or organizations sponsoring the advertisement. If the advertisement was paid for by the campaign, the ad should indicate "paid for by the campaign account of _____." If the advertisement was provided in-kind by a person or group, the ad should state "provided for in-kind by _____." If more than one person or group provided in-kind services in the production or broadcasting of the ad, the ad should so indicate.

Reference : Florida Statute 106.143(1)

Campaign Fund Raisers/Ticket Disclaimers

Any tickets or advertising for a campaign fund raiser must contain the statement, "The purchase of a ticket for, or a contribution to, the campaign fund raiser is a contribution to the campaign of (Name of candidate for whose benefit the campaign fund raiser is held)." Tickets must also contain the preceding political advertisement disclaimer information:

1. "Paid political advertisement" or "pd. pol. adv."
2. "Paid for by the campaign account of _____" or " Paid for in-kind by _____".
3. Political party affiliation or independent status.

Elections department resources

Political Campaign Signs

SECTION 33-99 OF THE METROPOLITAN DADE COUNTY CODE PROVIDES THE FOLLOWING REGULATIONS FOR POLITICAL CAMPAIGN SIGNS:

Section 33-99   Special Events Signs

(a) Regulations. Signs advertising special events, such as carnivals, concerts, public meetings, sports events, political campaigns or other uses of a similar nature shall be classified Class A temporary signs and shall not exceed twenty-two by twenty-eight inches in size except as to site of use, which shall be as hereinafter provided. Such signs shall not be closer than five feet to an official right of way and five feet to property under different ownership. Except as to site of use, which shall be as hereinafter provided the number of signs will be unlimited. Such signs shall be removed not later than thirty days after the special event or last election in which a candidate or issue was on the ballot.

(b) Responsibility for compliance. Promoters, sponsors and candidates shall be responsible for compliance with the provisions of this ordinance and shall remove signs promoting or endorsing their respective special events or candidacies when such signs are displayed or used in violation of this ordinance. Additionally, any private property owner who fails to remove an unlawful special events sign from his or her property shall be deemed in violation of this ordinance.

(c) Above provisions of this section which require the removal of signs shall be applicable to both the unincorporated and incorporated areas of Metropolitan Dade County, Florida.

Florida Voluntary Code of Fair Campaign Practices

As I seek public office in Florida, I honor the following principles as a guide to conduct which the public is entitled to expect of me:

1. I will address valid issues in my campaign, will tell the truth as to my intentions if I am elected and will fight fairly in any contest with my opponents.

2. I will shun demagoguery that seeks to deflect the public's attention to sham issues that obscure real concerns of the electorate.

3. I will limit my attacks on an opponent to legitimate challenges to that person's record, qualifications and positions.

4. I will neither use or permit the use of malicious untruths or scurrilous innuendoes about an opponent's personal life, nor will I make or condone unfounded accusations discrediting that person's integrity.

5. I will take personal responsibility for approving or disavowing the substance of attacks on my opponent that may come from third parties' supporting my candidacy.

6. I will not use or permit the use of campaign material that falsifies, distorts, or misrepresents facts.

7. I will neither use nor permit the use of last minute charges made without giving any opponent reasonable time in which to respond before election day.

8. I will neither use nor permit the use of appeals to bigotry in any form, and specifically to prejudice based on race, sex, sexual orientation, religion, or national origin.

9. I will demand that persons or organizations supporting me maintain these standards of fairness.

10. I will repudiate any abuses of this code.

Municipalities

When placing signs within a municipality, check with the City Clerk for information pertaining to municipal ordinances.

Municipal and Unincorporated Dade County Areas

Complaints pertaining to Signs on Private Property should be directed to the Dade County Building and Zoning Department at 375-2530.

Complaints regarding signs on Public Property (Right of Ways) should be directed to the Dade County Public Works Department (ENCO) at 375-2730 for enforcement.

Usage and Removal of Political Campaign Advertisements

1. Each candidate, whether for a federal, state, county, or district office, shall make a good faith effort to remove all of his political campaign advertisements within 30 days after:

   a. Withdrawal of his candidacy;

   b. Having been eliminated as a candidate; or

   Being elected to office.

   However, a candidate is not expected to remove those political campaign advertisements which are in the form of signs used by an outdoor advertising business as provided in Chapter 479. The provisions herein do not apply to political campaign advertisements placed on motor vehicles or to campaign messages designated to be worn on persons.

2. If political campaign advertisements are not removed within the specified period, the political subdivision has the authority to remove such signs and may charge the candidate the actual charge for such removal. Funds collected for removing such advertisement shall be deposited to the general revenue of the political subdivision.

3. Pursuant to Chapter 479, no political advertisements shall be erected, posted, painted, tacked, nailed or otherwise displayed, placed, or located on or above any state or county road right-of-way.

Reference: Florida Statute 106.1435

Elections department resources

Metropolitan Dade County
Supervisor of Elections Department
Absentee Ballot Request Policy

1. **By Phone** - An absentee ballot may be requested by the elector or a person representing the elector (limit of 3 requests per election) by calling the Absentee Ballot Section at 375-5858 with the following information:

   a. name of elector

   b. residence address

   c. address outside of Dade County where ballot is to be mailed (if applicable)

   d. elector's phone number

   e. date of birth

   f. place of birth

   g. social security number

   h. registration number (if available)

   i. reason for requesting an absentee ballot

   j. the dates of the elections for which an absentee ballot is needed.

2. **By Mail** - An absentee ballot may be requested by letter which contains the following information:

   a. name of elector

   b. residence address

   c. address where the ballot is to be mailed (if different)

   d. date of birth

   e. registration number (if available)

   f. reason for requesting an absentee ballot

   g. the dates of the elections for which an absentee ballot is needed

   h. signature of elector or electors, if the request is for more than one member of a family.

3. **In Person** - An absentee ballot can be voted in person at the Metro-Dade Elections Department's absentee ballot site at the lobby of the Stephen P. Clark Center, 111 NW 1st Street, or at one of the field sites set up during the week prior to each election. Call the Absentee Ballot Section at 375-5858 for times and locations.

4. **By a Third Party Pickup** - (Limit of 1 ballot per election) An absentee ballot may be picked up at the Metro-Dade Elections Department's absentee ballot site at the lobby of the Stephen P. Clark Center, 111 NW 1st Street, within 8 calendar days of the election by a person designated by the elector. A picture identification of the third party must be presented along with some form of identification from the elector (must include the elector's name, address and signature) and a written request containing the following information:

   a. name of person picking up the absentee ballot

   b. name of elector

   c. elector's phone number

   d. date of birth

   e. registration number (if available)

   f. reason for requesting an absentee ballot

   g. signature of elector.

Voter Solicitation Law

- **POLLING PLACE** - a polling place is defined as the building which contains the polling room where the ballots are cast.

- **SOLICITATION** - Solicitation includes, but is not limited to, seeking or attempting to seek any vote, fact, opinion, or contribution; distributing or attempting to distribute any political or campaign material, leaflet, or handout; conducting a poll; seeking or attempting to seek a signature on any petition; and selling or attempting to sell any item.

RESTRICTIONS

No person may solicit voters within 50 feet of the entrance to any Polling Place, on the day of any election. However, if there is a residence, established business, private property or park within 50 feet of the polling place, and that residence, established business, private property or park is different from the polling place, voters may be solicited on that property. Voters may also be solicited on public sidewalks and streets that fall within the 50-foot zone.

Example 1:

A park building is used as a polling place, and the park property extends 100 feet from the front entrance of the polling place. In this case, voters cannot be solicited within 50 feet of the entrance to the polling place.

Example 2:

A park building is used as a polling place and the park property extends 25 feet from the front entrance of the polling place. Property belonging to an apartment building begins 25 feet from the entrance of the park building. In this case, voters cannot be solicited within 25 feet of the entrance to the polling place, but can be solicited on the apartment building property.

Reference: Florida Statute 102.031

Elections department resources

4

Spreading the Word

Spreading the word to well-connected people is an important part of the groundwork in a successful campaign. The following plan worked for me.

About a year before the primary, I made a list of all the public officials, lawyers, doctors, business and labor people, teachers, lobbyists, homemakers, and heads of organizations I knew. I knew several of these people from the organizations to which I belong. Members of your church, PTA, or other civic groups are good resources. It took me several days to put together the list because I had to go over lists of everything in which I was ever involved. My list had over two hundred people on it, as I have been a part of my community for many years and my children went all through public school there.

I then prioritized the list in terms of people with money, people with influence, and people with time. Several people overlapped, but I assigned them a code and kept separate lists for each category. I included name, address, phone number, and notes about each person. It is a good idea to put the lists in alphabetical order because you will be using them over and over again. I then prioritized the names on each list with a number so that I could deal with the people who could offer the most help first. I met many people in their offices, but most I met at their homes, when they were relaxed and the whole family was around. This gave me the opportunity to talk to the spouse and to children who vote. At the meeting, I said I was running for the Florida House of Representatives and would welcome their support. I did not ask for anything more. I told them that I wanted them to learn about my candidacy from me, before they read about it in the paper. This was a courtesy call, and friends were very flattered that I took the time out to meet with them personally. I also took notes at each meeting and asked if there were any issues that they thought I needed to address.

When I got home, I transferred my notes about the meeting to a master list and used these records later for volunteers, fund-raising, and endorsements. I also sent a letter of thanks to every person I met as soon after the meeting as possible. I enclosed literature and an endorsement card. Obviously, I could not meet with all two hundred people, but I met with many and phoned the rest.

Six months later, I wrote a fund-raising letter using these names. By getting endorsements early, I was able to use these names in advertising and kept my opponents from using these key people. For the first few months, I was able to keep expenses extremely low. All of the money went for clerical help, postage, and printing.

Some candidates begin by holding a press conference and making a formal announcement to the local press. This is a terrific way to begin. The conference should be held at a central location at a time when the press is available. In the morning or at noon is a good time, as opposed to right before the evening news, when reporters are busy. Call all of your friends and ask them to be there so it will look like you already have support. For television or a newspaper picture, make it as colorful as possible. Have balloons, tee shirts, banners, or whatever else you can put together inexpensively. Make sure you are dressed for business. Women should put on extra makeup, as makeup tends to fade out on television and you want to appear as healthy as possible. Your message should be short, because radio and television depend upon "sound bites." Give the reasons why you are running and then ask for support. A week before the press conference, send a brief press release to all papers and radio and television stations. Include the short message and where and when your conference is being held. On the morning of the conference, it is a good idea to call the stations and papers and remind the reporters. If only one or two show up, the conference is still a success, because it is free publicity. Have someone there with a camera to take black-and-white photos that you can use in your publicity shots. I found that having a camera available throughout the campaign was a wonderful way to thank supporters with a picture and a great way to document the campaign. I used the pictures for many things later on in the campaign.

When I worked on presidential campaigns, I found that many of the same techniques were employed but on a much larger scale. For example, an advance person would move into a city and do the same things we did in my campaign. They would begin with a list of people to call and begin organizing people into the three categories (money, endorsements, and volunteers). They would work with the head of the political party once the primary was over and would appear at large meetings to "work the crowd."

Once I had my core supporters, who were old friends, and once I began to spread the word, I kept meeting new people. They rarely committed to supporting me right away, but weeks later those whom I had met early on would eventually support me over my opponent just because they felt they knew me.

- Make a list of all the people you know.

- Keep records of all meetings and people you phone for support.

- Follow up with letters of thanks, resumes, endorsements, and contribution cards.

5

Setting Up
Your Campaign
Headquarters

Your headquarters doesn't have to be glamorous and expensive, nor does it have to be a storefront on a major thoroughfare. It can be as humble as an unused room in your house. Madeline Kunin, former governor of Vermont, used her kitchen and other rooms in her house to begin her campaign for the state legislature. Several of my friends, including a county commissioner, turned their homes into campaign offices. I did too. My eldest daughter had gone off to law school, so I reclaimed her bedroom.

Fancy or simple, any location has its advantages and disadvantages. Ours being small, it was sometimes crowded but nonetheless always convenient to me. It was so small that we couldn't help but keep it neat and uncluttered, and that was certainly an advantage. All we had was a long couch, a tall bookcase with a built-in desk, two bridge tables, and a typewriter, which today would be replaced with a computer. I used the desk, the volunteer coordinator used one bridge table, and the manager used the other bridge table. We had three rotary phone lines installed, plus a separate one that I kept open for incoming calls. The bookcase was soon filled with boxes of index cards on all the voters in my district, arranged alphabetically by precinct. (It eventually looked like a card catalogue in a library.) Today, all of the lists of voters, which would be obtained from the elections department, would be in a computer file in precinct order by street number and in alphabetical order by district. If we needed volunteers to come in for special mailings, we used the kitchen and dining room tables, but those occasions were rare.

Many campaign activities are performed away from headquarters. For example, when it was time to call voters right before the election to remind them to vote, a friend loaned us his business office with twenty phone lines. The activity of standing along major thoroughfares holding campaign signs was organized at headquarters but obviously not conducted there. When it came to getting out and canvassing neighborhoods, the predominant activity in any district campaign, headquarters served only as a starting point or a place to drop off and pick up campaign materials. Basically, it is just a place where a few workers daily organize activities for the volunteers, a starting place for volunteers to begin an assignment, and a place to store your campaign paraphernalia.

A large storefront headquarters, the typical location from which most run a campaign, might be helpful if people walked in off the street to volunteer, but in my experience with other campaigns, this rarely happens. Unless there is a specific task that must be done regularly, volunteer are needed only on certain occasions and not all day long. The days of doing huge mailings at headquarters are gone; most candidates raise enough money to have mailings done professionally. If your district has more than a few thousand voters, preparing a mailing at headquarters becomes unwieldy. I have seen headquarters go unused day after day. A dark, quiet storefront headquarters can make a candidate look unpopular, so an out-of-the-way office may be a better choice after all. Just be sure your address and phone and fax numbers are on all your literature pieces. On the other hand, you do not want your headquarters so remote that people have trouble finding you. If you have a business office, perhaps you can set aside some space for a headquarters. Do whatever is convenient for the candidate.

I found it extremely helpful to be close to my office. I did not have to drive to get there. I could come home from work, change clothes, and immediately begin working on the campaign. My family, who were lukewarm about my candidacy at first, became very interested, indeed excited, as events began to unfold. They often helped when they weren't busy. Volunteers always had cold drinks and snacks available and even a TV when the work became tedious. The "rent" was certainly right. Best of all, when I was so wound up from the campaign that I had trouble falling asleep, I could work during the middle of the night without leaving the house.

When I first ran in 1986, I did not use a computer. I kept everything on 3 × 5 cards. The point is that it doesn't matter how you organize; it just matters that you be organized, whether on paper or electronically. Fundraising and canvassing generate much data, and you will need a system and a place to manage it all.

■ **Establish a campaign headquarters, keeping in mind comfort, proximity, and cost.**

■ Furnish the headquarters with enough desks, telephones and phone lines, a fax, a copier, and a computer. These can be purchased, leased, or borrowed. If you use more than one computer, they should be networked so data can be shared.

6

Setting Your Priorities

As the saying goes, "First things first." You can't win an election without taking the appropriate steps, and each step must be taken it its proper sequence. Speed also counts.

Here's a list of priorities that my staff and I followed. I stuck to this timetable for fourteen months, but if you don't have that kind of time, speed up the process.

The First Six Months
I. Fund-raising
    A. Find a treasurer
    B. Meet personally with potential contributors
    C. Send out fund-raising letters
    D. Follow up contributions with phone calls
II. Getting endorsements
    A. Meet with prominent members of the community
    B. Meet with influential leaders of constituencies (e.g., labor, education, environment)
    C. Meet with elected officials

III. Hire outside staff
  A. Hire a public relations and/or advertising consultant
    1. Create a budget for media
    2. Create a timetable for media
IV. Keep a calendar of events
  A. Find out where and when people in organizations meet
V. Research issues to create a platform
  A. Keep a record of issues important to your community
  B. Meet with experts on the issues
  C. Develop your position on these issues

The Last Six Months
I. Walk door to door
  A. Prepare a walking list by using a computer printout purchased from the elections department
  B. Have campaign literature, signs, and bumper stickers produced
  C. Buy a list of voters' phone numbers, and keep records of those you have met
  D. Contact volunteers for walking
II. Hire your volunteer coordinator
  A. Organize lists of volunteers for various activities
  B. Organize walks
  C. Organize phone bank
  D. Organize poll workers
  E. Organize election-day events
  F. Organize volunteer parties before and after election
III. Hire in-house staff (i.e., campaign manager, canvassing coordinator)
  A. Schedule appearances and events and manage calendar
  B. Help with questionnaires from interest groups
  C. Research speeches and answers to questionnaires

7

Raising Money

Raising money is the second most difficult exercise in running a campaign. Door-to-door canvassing is by far the most time-consuming as well as physically challenging component of any campaign. (Canvassing is discussed in Chapter 17.)

Even if you have never raised money before, you must learn how to do it effectively to have a good chance of winning. If you dislike the idea of asking people for money, get over it. Your opponents will ask for money and they will receive it. After my second term in office, I attended a campaign conference given by the Democratic Party. One of the featured speakers was an expert in political fund-raising. At the opening of his remarks, he said something so simple that I never forgot his words, "If you want money, you must *ask*."

Madeleine Kunin writes,

Until recently, lack of an independent income has kept many women from establishing a businesslike connection between power and money. What for many men is a normal bartering system is a new experience for most women...It runs contrary to most women's upbringing and instinct....One of the ironies of politics is that asking for money requires ego, but asking for increasingly large amounts of money requires submersion of ego....The political war chest is aptly named; it allows the candidate to go into battle. Each contribution not only enables one to pay staff and buy precious television time but success in fund-raising is in itself taken as a demonstration of political power. A candidate without money is not serious. A candidate who either is independently wealthy or raises large amounts of money automatically has to be reckoned with. Often a war chest itself will fend off opponents, like a nuclear deterrent. A good fund-raiser looks like a winner...The most effortless fund-raising occurs in the final days of a close race, when dollars pour in with no effort.

For years, I was involved in trying to put a cap on political spending through an organization called Common Cause. We felt that the emphasis on funds diminished the real issues in a campaign. We tried to institute a public/private match on contributions, which would mean that for every dollar raised by the candidate, a certain amount in public funds is made available. The plan would also limit the amount any one candidate could raise. The British have a very sane system, which is a cap on spending and three weeks to campaign.

So far, a cap has only worked at the presidential level and in some states for statewide races. The money comes from voluntarily checking off on your tax return a specified amount for political campaigns. The system has strict criteria for how the funds are matched and what the money can be used for.

The reality of a district legislative race is that money is very important, and the more you have, the easier it is to compete. Until the laws are changed, try to raise as much money as you can. The earlier you can raise it, the better.

Office	June	July	Aug.	Sept.	Oct.
a. Rent	$500	$500	$500	$500	$500
b. Equipment	In-kind contribution				
c. Phone	$500	$400	$500	$900	$900
deposit	$3,000				
d. Supplies	$200	$200	$200	$300	$300
e. Postage	$100	$100	$100	$400	$400
f. Volunteer Expenses	$200	$200	$200	$300	$300
Staff					
a. Manager	In-kind contribution				
b. Fundraiser	(see fundraising budget)				
c. Field Director	$2,000	$2,000	$2,000	$2,000	$2,000
d. Office Manager			$500	$500	$500
Printing					
a. Tabloid	$600		$600	$800	$600
b. Brochure				$600	
c. Leaflets			$200	$300	$300
d. Paraphernalia			$600	$300	
Fundraising	(see fundraising budget)				
Home Parties	In-kind contributions				
Direct Mail			$5,000	$9,000	$13,000
Phone Banks				$3,000	$3,500
a. Follow-up Mail				$4,000	$4,500
Volunteer Canvass	$500	$300	$400	$400	$500
Candidate Travel	$300	$200	$200	$200	$200

Sample budget and fund-raising projection for candidates provided by the National Democratic Party

	June	July	Aug.	Sept.	Oct.
Radio					
a. Production			$3,000		$3,000
b. Spot Buy				$13,500	$30,000
Get-Out-the-Vote					$6,000
Total Expenses	$4,930	$4,000	$3,600	$37,000	$66,450
Total Income	$38,500	$20,200	$5,000	$36,500	$37,500
Cash Flow	+33,570	+16,200	+1,400	-500.00	-28,590

SAMPLE FUNDRAISING PROJECTION

	June	July	Aug.	Sept.	Oct.
Candidate	$20,000 (loan)				
Clarke Family	$25,000	$6,000			
Finance Council (Solicitation of Prospects)		$3,000	$3,000	$26,000	$3,000
Events					
a. Allegra Roast				$6,000	
b. Reception #1	$4,000				
c. Lawyer's Lunch				$3,000	
d. Home Parties			$2,000	$3,000	$3,000
e. Reception # 2					$4,000
f. Two weeks to Go Party					$5,000
Direct Mail					
a. Proven Contributors Mail #1	$2,000	$6,000			
b. Proven Contributors Mail #2	$2,000		$5,000		
c. Proven Contributors Mail #3	$2,000		$4,500		

Sample budget and fund-raising projection for candidates provided by the National Democratic Party

	June	July	Aug.	Sept.	Oct.
d. Proven Contributors Mail #4	$2,000				$5,000
e. Proven Contributors "Over the Top" Appeal					$5,000
Political Action Committees					
a. Labor				$3,000	$13,000
b. Business				$600	$3,000
c. Other				$600	$2,000
Total (Gross)	$55,000	$9,000	$10,000	$46,550	$37,000
Fundraising Costs					
Program Costs	$4,000	$200	$2,500	$4,500	$5,000
Staff Costs	$2,500	$2,500	$2,500	$2,500	$2,500
Total (Net) **Cash Flow**	$48,500	$6,100	$5,000	$39,550	$29,500

Sample budget and fund-raising projection for candidates provided by the National Democratic Party

I began my fund-raising program by opening up a campaign checking account at a local bank. "Campaign Account of Susan Guber" was printed on the checks. To open the account, I wrote a check that was a loan from myself, which I could repay after the campaign was over. Some candidates choose to repay the loan, and others do not. I began my nest egg one year prior to the election. First, I mailed a letter to my list of prospective donors (many of whom I had met with to tell them that I was running), telling them why I chose to run and that a prerequisite for candidacy was money. I enclosed an endorsement card (see illustration) attached to a self-addressed envelope for checks to be returned. The card should include space for the contributor's name and

---

YES, I would like to help elect
★SUSAN GUBER★
to the Florida House

Name _____

Address _____

Phone _____ Occupation _____

I will:

_____ Walk and hand out literature

_____ Contribute financially, $ _____ enclosed.

_____ Make phone calls **This is your authorization to use**

_____ Host a party **my name in advertising.**

_____ Get sign locations

_____

Signature

Endorsement card

address as well as occupation (which many states require). Also get the contributor's phone and fax numbers, because those who contribute can be called upon to volunteer.

Once you mail the campaign letter to these people, money will not come pouring in, but you will have made people aware that you are running. Although you live and breathe the campaign, even your best friends need to be reminded that you are running, so keep telling people about the race. The next step is to call the people on your list and tell them you need donations. As you begin to receive checks, write your thank-you notes immediately. I cannot stress this strongly enough, not only because it is courteous to do so but because it generates goodwill. Enclose with the note a bumper sticker and notices of any upcoming events related to the campaign. One candidate enclosed a campaign newsletter; although not necessary, it is a nice touch. As friends volunteer to host fund-raisers, invite all contributors. Contributors are your best supporters because they are "investors" in your race.

Another successful way to raise money is to have your professional, labor, and business supporters write to their colleagues asking for money on your behalf. Draft a letter for your supporters to use on their own stationery. If you draft and process the letter and stuff and mail the envelopes, then all your supporter has to do is sign the letter. By asking little of the supporter and doing all of the work yourself, you will ensure that the letter actually gets distributed. Too many campaigns rely on the good intentions of volunteers and leave too much to chance. The more of the campaign that you control through the campaign office, the more that will get accomplished.

I also used this idea with organizations that do not endorse candidates, such as the League of Women Voters. I sent out a letter signed by four past presidents asking for money. I used mailing lists from the League of Women Voters and other women's organizations for the presidents' letters. Tailor your letter to appeal to the group you are soliciting (e.g., a chamber of commerce needs a pro-business letter). Not all mail leads to money; some leads to volunteers and some leads to votes—the ultimate support.

The advantage of early fund-raising is that in six to eight months, you can go back to the *same people* and ask for more. People do not seem to mind giving again! The observable results of fund-raising, such as radio and newspaper ads, brochures, signs on benches, and bumper stickers, make your supporters aware that you are credible, and they become even more enthusiastic. Several friends called me when they saw my bus bench signs. Their enthusiasm for assisting both financially and personally was all the greater.

Money raised far in advance of an election may keep some opponents from running altogether. If you have $30,000 six months before an election, any opposition would have to raise $30,000 just to get where you already are. Meanwhile, you are out raising more! Raising money early frees you to do other campaign work. You can be out walking door to door when others are having their first fund-raisers.

Money begets money. It's an old political rule that financial support sends potential opponents a message that you are a major contender and that you intend to win.

By the time the community at large was aware I was running, I had banked $50,000 in certificates of deposit to be used in the last month of my campaign, when I would need it most. All the early funds were from individual contributors, in small amounts, as opposed to corporate checks. Our treasurer's report was so fat that we had to file it in four separate files. By law, anyone has access to your list of contributors because you must file a copy with the elections department quarterly. It is intimidating to opponents to see page after page with names of people who are committed enough to give you money. It is even more nerve-wracking if those contributors live in the district and, of course, will vote for you. Campaign language is the same language used to describe war. Words such as strategy, war chest, and campaign are all taken from battles. Part of it is psychological, and it is particularly unnerving for an opponent to see so many people and so much money committed to you.

In the month before an election, if organizations with political action committees endorse your candidacy, they will send money. It is foolhardy for a first-time candidate to count these groups because they want to see how serious you are. By raising money, you will prove your worth. Therefore, do not count on PAC funds in the beginning.

I had two primary elections. If you do well in the first primary, money flows in for the second. If you win the second, money flows in for the general election. You may have to send out another mailing and call people again, but the good news is that you will never have to work as hard to keep the momentum going. People love to support a winner! By winning, you have become a proven commodity. The day of each of my primaries, we had a fund-raising letter ready to be mailed as soon as the television commentators announced my victory. Frank, my campaign manager, dropped the mail off at the central post office before midnight the day of each election. We were going to need the new money fast. Three days later, people were bringing in checks and mail was pouring into head-quarters. In Florida, there is only three weeks between the primaries, and you need money instantly. The media, for example, want the money and the ad copy well in advance of the election. I had managed to save a little money from the first primary, but by being organized and having that contributor letter ready to go, I quickly raised more. Aggressive fund-raising is a necessity if you intend to win—and no one intends to lose!

Having a party to raise campaign funds was more difficult for me and not as productive as a mailing. The work that is involved in throwing the party is time consuming unless it is a turnkey operation. If a friend says he or she will take care of the whole event, from invitations to cleanup, and all your campaign staff must do is have you attend, then it is well worth the hour or two of your time. I have been to many fund-raisers where there were only a handful of contributors and very little money was raised. However, Florida State Senator Helen Gordon Davis tells of a unique event that brought her much money in her first race:

> The most fun-filled and successful fund raising activity I ever held was my first in 1974. Fifty households had parties for my candidacy at their homes—simultaneously—on the same night. Each host was responsible for preparing his own guest list and supplying his own food and refreshments.
>
> Some hosts, particularly students at the university, charged a dollar per person and served hot dogs and

sodas. Some charged $100 per couple and had catered affairs. Each person could start any time but had to end by 9:00 p.m. I did not personally attend any of these. At nine o'clock all the guests converged at a mammoth reception hall where there were various desserts and drinks and an orchestra. Balloons were flying, booths were built and T-shirts with "Elect Helen Gordon Davis" on them were sold at a two dollar profit each, as were cards disseminated and filled out with volunteer checks on them.

We had over 1,000 people there and each person had a financial stake in my election. This was my first announcement as a candidate for the State Legislature-and the spirit of friendship, the dancing and frivolity, were only exceeded by the enthusiasm demonstrated for my candidacy. The press gave us great coverage and thus my campaign was launched with a beginning $20,000 fund and lots and lots of volunteers.

So try fund-raising parties, by all means. If they work, you may be in for a windfall.

If you have potentially big contributors, it helps to meet them personally in their office or home. I received checks from 95% of the people I took the time to meet. The check was rarely given to me at that meeting but usually followed a letter or a phone call. When people ask how much to give, assess what you think they would be comfortable with. If I knew a person could well afford the maximum, which was $1,000, I would say that the maximum per election is $1,000. Be appropriate; a banker can give a few hundred dollars whereas a teacher could be safely asked to give $50.

I was very lucky in finding a treasurer. A friend of mine is a Certified Public Accountant, head of a large firm, and has been a treasurer for other candidates. He was happy to take on this responsibility. He and his secretary prepared all of the contributor reports and paid all of the bills incurred by the campaign. I had only to collect the checks and send them to him daily. Toward the end of the campaign, we hired high school students with cars to pick up checks from contributors, drop off checks at the treasurer's office, or to pay bills. This last item was important, as most vendors to political campaigns demand payment before the goods are delivered or COD. Many vendors say that candidates notoriously do not pay bills and therefore are careful to protect themselves.

If you know a CPA, ask him or her to consider the job. I included my treasurer's name on all campaign literature, including the bus bench signs. It was a small way of saying thanks for all the work he had to do. You can use anyone who is willing to read the law pertaining to campaign treasurers and is meticulous and conscientious. It is one job that you should not take on yourself or give to a person who is cavalier about it. It is a major commitment to the campaign and you can be fined for not doing things properly. In my last campaign, when I ran for the Florida Senate, the 1992 hurricane in Dade County prevented most candidates from getting their treasurers' reports in on time. Computers were down for a month. The whole city was gridlocked. Tallahassee, which is 600 miles away, was slow to understand our plight. I was fined $50 a day for every day the report was late. At the time, we were interested in survival; the last thing anyone cared about was the report. Months later, the state voided all of the fines, but it literally took an act of God to accomplish.

Having a great treasurer helps you to deal with these issues. That is why money is so crucial. The more you take in, the more you can contract out. If you have money, you can pay an accountant to do the job. The candidate needs to focus on raising money and being visible wherever there are voters. Subcontracting the "housekeeping" chores is a wise use of money.

STATE OF FLORIDA
APPOINTMENT OF CAMPAIGN TREASURER
AND DESIGNATION OF CAMPAIGN DEPOSITORY
FOR CANDIDATES
(Section 106.021(1), F.S.)

(PLEASE TYPE)

CHECK APPROPRIATE BOX

☐ Original Appointment

☐ Deputy Treasurer

☐ Reappointment of Treasurer

☐ Secondary Depository

Name of Candidate	1. Address (include post office box or street, city, state, zip code)

Telephone (optional)	2. Party (**Partisan candidates only**)	3. Office (add district, circuit or group number)

I have appointed the following person to act as my   ☐ Campaign Treasurer   ☐ Deputy Treasurer

4. Name of Treasurer or Deputy Treasurer

5. Mailing Address (if post office box or drawer add street address)	6. Telephone

7. City	8. County	9. State	10. Zip Code

I have designated the following named bank as my   ☐ Primary Depository   ☐ Secondary Depository

11. Name of Bank	12. Street Address

13. City	14. County	15. State	16. Zip Code

I WILL NOTIFY YOU OF ANY ADDITIONS OR CHANGES TO THESE APPOINTMENTS.

17. Signature of Candidate	Date
X	

Campaign Treasurer's Acceptance of Appointment

I, _____, do hereby accept the appointment as
(Please Print or Type)

☐ Campaign Treasurer   ☐ Deputy Treasurer for the campaign of _____,

who is seeking nomination or election as a _____ candidate to the office of
(Party)

_____. As a duly registered voter in _____

County, Florida, I am qualified to accept this appointment.

_____	X _____
Date	Signature of Campaign Treasurer or Deputy Treasurer

Campaign treasurer's report

FLORIDA DEPARTMENT OF STATE, DIVISION OF ELECTIONS

CAMPAIGN TREASURER'S REPORT SUMMARY

(1) _____ (2) _____
Candidate, Committee or Party Name   I.D. Number

(3) _____
Address (number and street)   City   State   Zip Code

☐ Check box if address has changed since last report

(4) Check appropriate box(es):

☐ Candidate (office sought): _____

☐ Political Committee   ☐ Check if PC has DISBANDED

☐ Committee of Continuous Existence   ☐ Check if CCE has DISBANDED

☐ Party Executive Committee

(5) REPORT IDENTIFIERS

Cover Period: From ____/____/____ To ____/____/____   Report Type _____

☐ Original   ☐ Amendment   ☐ Special Election Report   ☐ Independent Expenditure Report

(6) CONTRIBUTIONS THIS REPORT	**(7) EXPENDITURES THIS REPORT**
Cash & Checks $__,____,____.____	Monetary Expenditures $__,____,____.____
Loans $__,____,____.____	Transfers to Office Account $__,____,____.____
Total Monetary $__,____,____.____	Total Monetary $__,____,____.____
In-kind $__,____,____.____	**(8)** Other Distributions $__,____,____.____

(9) CERTIFICATION

It is a first degree misdemeanor for any person to falsify a public record (ss. 839.13, F.S.)

I certify that I have examined this report and it is true, correct and complete	I certify that I have examined this report and it is true, correct and complete
_____	_____
Name of ☐ Treasurer ☐ Deputy Treasurer	Name of ☐ Candidate ☐ Chairman (PC/PTY Only)
X _____	X _____
Signature	Signature

Campaign treasurer's report

CAMPAIGN TREASURER'S REPORT – ITEMIZED CONTRIBUTIONS

(1) Name _____ (2) I.D. Number _____

(3) Cover Period ____/____/____ through ____/____/____ (4) Page _____ of _____

(5) Date / (6) Sequence Number	(7) Full Name (Last, First, Suffix, Middle) Street Address & City, State, Zip Code	(8) Contributor		(9) Contribution Type	(10) In-kind Description	(11) Amendment	(12) Amount
		Type	Occupation				
/ /							
/ /							
/ /							
/ /							
/ /							
/ /							
/ /							
/ /							

Campaign treasurer's report

In short, start early and raise plenty. You can never have too much, and in the unlikely event you do, you can give it to a charity or even give it back to the contributors. That makes a great impression and confirms that you are a fiscally responsible candidate.

- Make a list of all businesses, community leaders, interest groups, and individuals who may be able to contribute.

- Personally visit with each one of the above.

- Send a letter from yourself or from a group leader asking for money. Include a contribution envelope in the mailing.

- Have others organize fund-raising events.

- Thank all contributors personally and promptly.

- Maintain with the treasurer records of all money collected.

8

Hiring Staff

I tried to hire staff who would complement my own personality and talents. I was lucky that my daughter Elizabeth graduated from college six months prior to the election and became my volunteer coordinator. One advantage was that she is outgoing and another is that she knew many of my friends. She is very organized and did a good job running the daily operation. After we won the primary, she hired an assistant to help get volunteers for the walks, phone bank, and polls. A cheerful, organized person is important in that capacity.

The best way to find staff is to look for people in community organizations with which you are involved. Try to identify or ask for people who share your concerns, are conscientious, and have interpersonal skills. It may be someone who works full time and can come to your headquarters several evenings a week. Most campaigns begin with evening work; perhaps you can encourage someone to begin a few nights a week as a volunteer. If that person is dedicated and works well with you, then you can offer him or her a position after you collect some money.

That is how Frank Morra began as my assistant. I had seen him for years working as a volunteer and then as staff on other campaigns. He had a full-time job but was willing to begin volunteering evenings after work. In September 1985, one year prior to the first primary, we began by putting together our first fund-raising letter. After we obtained a bulk mail permit, we stuffed two hundred envelopes (on the floor of my living room) with letters asking for money. Frank also obtained an enlarged street map of our area from a local bookstore. Armed with the map and the voter list from the elections department, he was then able to create "walking routes" that we could use in our door-to-door canvassing. He had lived in town his whole life and knew his way around the district.

However, most of the campaign work was subcontracted out of headquarters. Today, with fax capability, that is even easier to do. Our treasurer worked from his own offices, and his secretary was always ready to give us a daily tally of the money we raised. At first, I paid my own business secretary overtime and had her type my thank-you letters and resume. (I used my resume before I had money for real campaign literature.)

Mostly, however, I began the process alone and realized what kind of help I would need. I needed a public or political relations person to write brochures and advertisements, and I hired one of the leading people in the county, Dick Rundell, and later Bob Levy. He did some research as well, on specific subjects about which I had little knowledge. If I were asked by an organization to write a column for their newsletter, he would gather facts and background and prepare the statement for my approval. A good political publicist can sense and help you avoid potential trouble, too. I was always very candid about my views on issues. My publicist would appear at the places I was asked to speak and warn me about a particular group so that I would not say something that was abhorrent to them. His critique of my speeches and how well the group received me was valuable as well.

A good publicist is important. A publicist's job is to apportion the advertising budget, which is the bulk of your campaign budget, and decide where it can best be spent. Most big cities have excellent political public relation firms. Many specialize according to party affiliation. In small towns, you can hire a local general advertising agency.

My publicist's first piece of advice to me was that television was a waste of money in a district race. It was expensive to produce and even more expensive to buy prime air time. Moreover, television scatters the message countywide, and I needed to target the district. For countywide or rural campaigns, television is the best medium, and your publicist should help you with it, but for me, direct mailings were the best form of advertising.

Hire the publicist early in the race, because most have a set fee for an entire campaign. As a result, you can have their expertise for a full year if you need it. One of the advantages of getting into the race early is that you can tie up the best publicist, thereby keeping your opponents from getting to him or her first. Again, the psychological aspect of the race comes into play.

I also hired a direct mail company. The woman who owned this business worked out of her house and did newsletter mailings for organizations. We provided her with our voter list from the elections department, which was delivered to her on a magnetic disk. She could then prepare mailings, get them to the post office, and guarantee arrival before election day.

After four months, the local medical association and labor unions endorsed me through their political action committees (PACs). PACs are registered under election law to collect money for candidates through their members. Both of these organizations decided to give me an in-kind contribution of staff support. That provided me with extra help for walking, mailing, and phoning.

The full-time staff in my first race consisted of two people—the volunteer coordinator and the canvassing coordinator. Others who were on the payroll were part time or were hired for a particular event. As so often happens, I hired one of them to run my legislative office after I won the election.

- ■ After laying the groundwork for your campaign by yourself, begin looking for the types of coordinators you will need.

- ■ Identify volunteers or local activists who could serve as part-time or full-time staff.

- ■ Ask elected officials and party chiefs for the names of companies that handle public relations and mailings for candidates.

9

Defining the Issues

Having served as an aide to a county commissioner and a state representative, I had a basic knowledge of local and state issues. I had also been a member of some clubs, such as Common Cause, the League of Women Voters, the Sierra Club, and the Chamber of Commerce. Civic associations are helpful in framing the issues for your community. They explore and evaluate ideas before coming to a consensus. The membership can then publicize the opinions of the group. Even if you are unable to attend most meetings, their newsletters provide you with information regarding their current activities. Your local phone book lists all such community organizations.

The best way to find out about current issues, when community meetings take place, and who is in a leadership position is through the local paper. Even the free community newspapers that are available around town are helpful. For a federal office, the *Washington Post, New York Times,* and *Wall Street Journal* are valuable.

I maintained a file of news articles to use as background for speeches. An accordion file with separate slots for the issues was perfect. I kept the file up to date by cleaning it out as soon as new articles appeared. Then, when I needed to write a speech, I had the latest documents at my fingertips. My file was broken down into education, crime, environment, economic development, healthcare, and general issues.

I also kept a card file on people I met. It consisted of their business cards, filed by issue as well. If I needed an expert to advise me on an issue or to help fill out a candidate questionnaire, the cards were a handy tool that saved valuable time.

It took a few weeks for me to decide what the important issues were to my voters. I would ask people as I met with them, went to meetings, or started to go door to door. It was interesting to see the reaction I would get from some. People could get very angry when talking about the issues. I had to remain neutral and just listen to their views. Stay composed and do not get involved in an argument.

You will slowly gain an understanding of the issues. Keep an open mind, Many issues are complex but do not demand an opinion from you immediately. It takes time to develop an understanding of the issues, so do not feel you need to be an expert right away. Also, the important issues may change, so keep listening.

Four issues emerged and stayed pretty much the same in the three terms that I ran for office. One year crime was emphasized, one year education, and another year healthcare. In my last term, it was water quality, because a dry cleaner had leaked toxic waste and it infiltrated the water supply. This was an emergency and tied up our office with anxious citizens for months. If there is one issue on which everyone is focused, you can call for a public hearing and get all the parties together at a meeting. It could help solve the problem and will help you emerge as a leader and problem solver.

When I was invited to speak to an audience, I found

Pitch an issue that needs attention

out which of my key issues stood out as the most important and, of course, emphasized that one. If no one introduces you before a campaign speech, always state your name and the boundaries of the district. Don't speak for more than five minutes. You would rather have people wanting to hear more instead of boring them. If several candidates speak, try to be either first or last; those are the ones that are remembered. Candidates speak at times when people are trying to relax, and listening to issues can be work, so say what you have to say as succinctly as possible. If you can weave in an appropriate anecdote or relate to the group in some way, so much the better. And always thank the audience for coming.

When I first decided to run, I thought I would have to research many issues, develop position papers on each one, and become an expert on all. Not true. People asked the same questions over and over again. All I needed to know was a little more than the audience knew. People want a simple direct answer; they do not want to be snowed under with too much information, statistics, or big words.

If you are asked a question that you haven't thought about, say so and say you will find the answer. If you get back to the person who asked the question, I guarantee he or she will be a supporter. If you are undecided, say so. Explain that you need more information. If you are on the unpopular side of an issue, don't lie about your beliefs. Even an uninformed audience will be able to sense dishonesty, and you will lose all credibility. Oftentimes, a particularly controversial issue is not even raised. Don't draw attention to it! I was never asked about the death penalty, so I never had to deal with an unpopular position on it. Be honest; it is the easiest and best policy.

Fuller Warren, governor of Florida in 1948, writes in *How to Win in Politics* about the need for truthfulness on the campaign trail: "I recommend taking a positive and unequivocal position on all pertinent issues. I am well aware that fence-straddling is favored by some successful politicians, but I know it is not the right way and seems seldom to be the winning way."

Thus, the issues are important but are emphasized much less on the trail than you might imagine. The truth is that it is more a matter of how you look, your media image, and how many homes you have time to walk to.

- **Read newspapers, watch TV, and listen to the radio.**

- **Familiarize yourself with local issues. Keep an up-to-date clippings file.**

■ Ask people what issues are important.

■ Watch for key issues to emerge.

■ Interview "experts" on these key issues.

■ Develop your platform from all the information you have accumulated.

■ Keep the number of key issues to a minimum.

10

Writing and Delivering Speeches

Ever since I can remember, I have been terrified of public speaking! My fear was pathological. I would go to any extreme to avoid it. I was so nervous that I was even afraid to ask a question of a public speaker when I was a member of an audience. My heart would begin to pound and I would freeze. I can remember having that feeling when I became program chair of Common Cause in 1978. Part of my responsibility was to introduce the guest of the evening. I devised a way to avoid dealing with this "dreaded" task by designating a master of ceremonies or having the president open the meeting. A year later, I found myself the master of ceremonies for the winners of a countywide student cultural arts competition called the New World Festival of the Arts. The event was the culmination of a whole year's work on my part in coordinating a countywide project. Since I originated the project, I was expected to say a few words. Indeed, my name was on the program! I was such a nervous wreck that when I arrived at the podium, I spoke so quickly that no one understood a word I said. Obviously, I was trying to get the ordeal behind me.

I realized that the fear of speaking before an audience was preventing me from achieving what I wanted to do in life. As you join organizations and begin to work for them, keep in mind that the best way to become known is through public speaking. You can reach dozens more people through a speech than you can one on one. If you have something urgent to talk about, then you can reach even more people via the media.

I obviously had to overcome this fear if I wanted to run for office. How did I deal with this anxiety? I did it by taking small steps. The first step I took was to find a public speaking course that would not be intimidating. I had heard of Dale Carnegie and decided to attend a class. Every large city in the world has a Dale Carnegie school. They are listed in the phone book. I called to find out when the next set of classes would meet. Deciding to go to that first class was one of the most courageous things I have ever done. When I opened the door and saw all those people sitting there waiting for the instructor, I took the seat closest to the door (in case I wanted a quick getaway). When the class began, the instructor asked each person to stand up and give their name. I had no problem with that. The instructor then asked students to come to the front of the class in groups of four and tell a little about themselves. As the time approached for my team, my heart began to pound. I seriously thought of leaving. But then I was overcome with a greater fear—that the instructor would see me trying to escape and call out, "Ms. Guber why are you leaving?" Eventually I did make it to the front of the class. I spoke clearly and gained some confidence. It helped to know about the subject— myself. I felt better with each tiny success, because I knew how important these skills were to my future. For me, it was life or death for any career in public office.

Six anxious weeks later, I received a diploma and the award for being the best speaker in the class! My final speech lasted two whole minutes. To my joy, I never passed out or made a complete fool of myself. Fifteen years later, I still run into friends from that class. The course gave me the strength I needed to get on my feet and speak, plus the reward of hearing an audience applaud. If you suffer from stage fright, a course such as this will help you to overcome it.

Part of my fear arose from not knowing what to say, how to say it, or how to prepare a speech. The course taught me to speak on a subject I know about, prepare myself without memorizing, speak with enthusiasm, and make eye contact. As the instructor emphasized, the only way to overcome the fear is to force yourself to give a speech.

My next public speaking course was at the local community college. When I started the class, I found out that I was the only one with prior experience, so I felt pretty smug. The other students in class were so nervous that one lady, upon seeing the camera used to videotape speakers, left in tears. It brought back painful memories. The advantage of this course was that each speaker was videotaped and the tapes were replayed for analysis by the class. When I saw the tapes, I understood that people do not always show the nervousness they may feel. My video helped me understand myself as others see me, and I was happy to see that it was not so bad. It was a fabulous teaching tool. I learned that I needed to speak slowly and make eye contact. Find out if the adult education program in your community offers a class such as this.

Once I finished the two classes, I wanted to continue to practice speaking in front of an audience. My goal was to speak as often as I could. I asked my instructor and classmates what to do next. They repeatedly mentioned a club called Toastmasters International, which is a world-wide club of dues-paying members. It was listed in the phone book in several places, as there were many chapters in Miami alone. The club is extremely well organized, and most meetings are listed in the local paper. Again, I had to push myself to go. The old fear returned, as I expected these folks to be professional speakers. Having a tooth extracted seemed like an easier exercise. Even giving birth looked less painful. But to my surprise, the first meeting was fun and *no one called upon me to speak.* I was a visitor, and the president simply acknowledged that I was there. I also realized that I could learn some great new skills, including how to chair a meeting, speak impromptu, deliver a seven-minute speech, give directions publicly, perform as a master of ceremonies, tell a joke, and critique another speaker. The exercises covered everything I would ever need as an elected official. The meetings were beautifully organized and lasted only an hour. Upon paying dues, I was given a manual. Each progressive chapter provided instructions for a more demanding speech. By the time I was halfway through the book, I had all the confidence I needed. That is not to say that I did not sweat out each speech, but each speech was progressively more difficult to prepare, which is a logical plan for learning. I would write out a speech and then rewrite key phrases. I would practice in front of the mirror each night for a week. I also used a tape recorder and a clock. I would practice my speech while I went running in the late afternoon. Soon the speech was a part of me, and I had nothing to be anxious about. By not memorizing, I could think my way through the key points and begin to ad-lib.

It is said that for each minute you speak, twenty minutes goes into preparation. For most people, public speaking is not a skill bestowed at birth; it is cultivated through experience. As with anything, some people have an easier time with public speaking than others. (Jessie Jackson, I believe, was born with this gift.) The only way to learn is to get up before an audience. It is the best practice you can have. Take it from a former coward—it gets easier with each talk.

Watch good orators and notice how they open with an interesting idea, make eye contact, and move their body with the words. They have a theme, they pause appropriately, and they use the names of members of their audience when they make a point that applies to them. They also try to smile and look as if they are enjoying themselves. That relaxes them and the audience as well. To close, a good speaker will be brief while summarizing what he or she has said. Speaking effectively involves conveying interesting information, acting, and entertaining, all at once. The more speaking I did, the more I was able to weave old speeches into new ones, and that helped cut down on preparation time.

I will never be an expert. Each time I speak, I privately pat myself on the back and remember when I was terrified at the thought of standing up in front of a group. The truth is that I was not prepared, and the difference is that now I am.

My last speech at Toastmasters was my best. It was a year before election day. I had won a speaking contest, and my spirits soared. It was at that meeting that I knew I was ready to run for public office. I announced at the end of the speech that I was a candidate for the Florida House of Representatives. Club members had no idea that I was going to run for office. They jumped to their feet and gave me a standing ovation. For the past six years, I had worked to try to overcome my speaking phobia, and I finally had the confidence I needed. That night was a milestone for me, and I shared it with my fellow Toastmasters.

After Toastmasters, I tried to keep two speeches

handy. One was a political speech and one was a generic speech on lobbying techniques. I kept both current so that if I was called upon to speak, I would be ready. Speaking well before an audience is a politician's bread and butter. A well thought-out and delivered talk will gain you recognition, credibility, and ultimately votes.

The route I took to becoming comfortable with public speaking is but one way to success. One woman told me she conquered her fear by taking notes and watching others as they spoke. She then incorporated her observations into her own speeches. She forced herself to talk before an audience. The more she spoke, the more confident and effective a speaker she became. Another woman told me that as a child, she was encouraged to speak before large family gatherings. Thus, she was never nervous as an adult. Still another person suggested that I try deep breathing and relaxation exercises just before I came to the podium. Whatever you choose, you need to begin somewhere. Start by asking questions as a member of an audience, then offer to introduce or moderate a panel, and then jump in and give a short speech.

- Public speaking, as a method of getting your message across, is a vital skill to learn.

- Learn how community programs can help you master the art of public speaking.

- Ask good speakers how they started out, and watch them for ideas on how to handle yourself effectively.

11

Finding and Using Volunteers

F rank, my campaign manager, often said, "Volunteers are like gold," and it is so true. They are a treasure. People who give up a Saturday morning for your campaign will be engraved on your heart and you will never forget them. We tried to find projects for volunteers that would not be tedious and that had a beginning and an end. It is important for volunteers to feel that they are accomplishing a job. It is also important for them to understand what they are doing and how it fits into the big campaign picture. We tried to keep stuffing envelopes to a minimum. By raising money, you will be able to hire a service and take mailings outside of headquarters. Contributor solicitations (which were less than 1,000 pieces of mail) were processed with volunteers in less than an hour.

Most of the projects had to do with walking to homes, manning phone banks, and poll watching the day of the election. All of the projects involved direct contact with voters, and all had a two-hour commitment. That is how we were able to keep our volunteers fresh and eager to help again. Elizabeth, the volunteer coordinator, reviewed the contribution envelopes on which people indicated they could volunteer time and built a volunteer base. As she used volunteers, she asked if they could bring a friend, an adult child, or a spouse the next time. She always tried to secure another commitment when they finished their task. To get more help, she spoke before the groups that supported me and asked for volunteers at their meetings. Two months prior to the election, she had a list of 127 people. Not all were "regulars," but many did return to volunteer several times. If you are endorsed by a group such as nurses, teachers, or labor unions, the members will frequently sign up to volunteer as a group, although this doesn't happen often for first-time candidates. These groups of people should be treated the same as your other volunteers. Have them work on your campaign out of your headquarters, because you will need to have control over their activities. You do not want them to repeat the work you are doing, nor do you want them to do anything that could harm your campaign (such as destroying other candidates' signs).

Each evening after dinner, Elizabeth would get on the phone and call the volunteers. Realizing that she would be spending hours on the phone, we purchased a headset telephone for her. She had a large calendar (today this task would be computerized) and she would sign people up to help out an evening or two a week. Elizabeth was always cheerful on the phone and expressed her thanks when she got an affirmative answer from a volunteer. We found that it took thirty phone calls to get eighteen people to agree to come, and then sometimes only twelve would actually show up. The day of the appointment, she would call and leave a message to remind them of the commitment.

For six months, volunteers came to headquarters each night and twice daily on weekends to gather for the door-to-door walks. When volunteers arrived, they were greeted by either Frank, Elizabeth, or myself. Everything for the

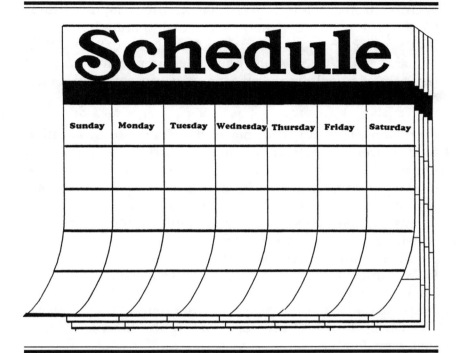

walk was ready, and we explained the program. New volunteers were given someone to work with who had done the project before. We supplied water jugs and mosquito repellent (a must in South Florida) as well as the checklists and literature.

Although the walks were structured in two-hour time blocks, we explained that if any volunteers needed to finish early, they could just bring the materials back and leave them on my doorstep. Elizabeth was usually there making more calls, but some nights she would join in the canvassing.

By the time election day rolled around, many of the volunteers had become like family. They had walked, phoned, poll watched, and donated many hours of their valuable time. They had covered the whole district of over 85,000 voters! Apartment dwellers were blitzed with "literature drops." Material was left at their doors without ringing the bell. We visited every single-family home that had a voter and followed up with a phone call. It was a massive effort that would have been impossible without the help of a well-organized team of volunteers and a staff coordinator. Make this operation a priority.

Former Congressman Dante Fascell provided a "lit-drop" for all members of his party. That was in addition to our work. He took all of the candidates' campaign literature and put together a package, with his literature at the top. It was nice to be tied in to such a prestigious person, but don't count on your congressman, your party, or anyone else. This has to be your effort, and no one else will take the time to do it for you.

Three days before the election, we had a special project for volunteers: distributing all our remaining literature. They were asked to take a stack of literature and go house to house to their neighbors and remind them to vote.

On each of the three election nights, the victory parties were for the volunteers as well as the candidate. We had lots of food, drinks, decorations, and TV sets. A month after the general election, I had a big catered dinner for the volunteers and contributors. It was my small way of saying thanks for a job very well done. I even gave out clocks that said, "Thanks for your time." My volunteers gave me a plaque that said, "Congratulations, From the Campers at Camp Guber." It was fun, and many enjoyed being a part of a winning team.

- **Hire a volunteer coordinator.**

- **Cultivate a group of volunteers.**

- **Plan how you will use the volunteers.**

- **Never tire or overuse volunteers.**

- **Thank volunteers in an appropriate way.**

12

Exploring and Utilizing New Technology

When I wrote the first version of this book in 1987, the information that was collected by the elections department was mostly raw data. It gave a person's party affiliation, address, gender, ethnicity, and voting history. Also available was a list in zip code order for mailing, walking order for door-to-door canvassing, or alphabetical order for keeping records. Today, data in computers include everything from income, religion, ethnicity, and level of education to what a person does for a living. You can now get a more sophisticated look at the people in the district in which you are running because technology has made the information readily available. Bear in mind, however, that because populations change, there could be a difference in the makeup of an area from one election to the next. In Dade County, Florida, for example, there was a massive influx of immigrants from Cuba in 1980 which changed the population and voting patterns over the next few years. It amounted to a complete shift from Anglo to Latino and Democrat to Republican.

There are many companies that will take elections data and customize it for your purposes. For instance, if you are running in a primary, you can get a list of Democrats or Republicans who voted in certain elections, who are in a certain age group, who have a certain income, and who are of a certain ethnic background. Those may be the people you want to target first, because they vote your party and they vote faithfully. You then can visit, phone, or send a special letter to these people first. This helps tremendously if you are running in an enormous area and you only have time to work key areas that you know will vote for you.

If money is no object, and that is rare in a first race, you may want to hire a company to poll the area to find out what kind of people vote and what issues are important. A good pollster will ask about other candidates in the district and can then gauge pretty accurately their level of name recognition and how favorably they are perceived. After my first two primaries, and after I had walked the whole district, my name recognition factor was 33 out of 100%. I was deflated because I had thought that everyone would know me. As it turned out, that number was high; it meant that one out of three people in the district had heard of me! The next highest candidate had a recognition factor of 18%. When you consider that all you need is one more vote than your opponent, I was doing well. Polls are extremely expensive, and this one was a gift from a lobby group provided as an in-kind contribution. Polls can give you a false sense of security. If you think you are ahead, you may not work as hard. In an election for an open seat, few people will know any of the candidates anyway. I had a sense of the type of people who would be voting because I had lived in the area for years and figured I "looked like the district." People were mostly middle class, white, well educated, and politically central. Polling can be very helpful in a second race, when you will probably have more money. It gives you a report card in terms of what the voters think of you after your first term in office. It tells you what issues to stress, your level of name recognition versus your opponent, and how favorably your name is viewed. In the whole scheme of a first campaign, a poll could be on your wish list but is not an essential item.

In 1993, hailed as the "year of the woman," I ran for the Florida Senate. Because the district was 300 miles long, and was obviously too big to walk, I purchased data specifically on all women who voted in the last two Democratic primaries and the last presidential election. This eliminated women who rarely voted but who were still on the voting rolls. I also purchased all of the phone numbers of this group of women. Every night, instead of walking, my volunteers and I phoned these women and told them that I was the only woman running in the race and that I hoped they would support me. Many were surprised to get a call from the candidate herself. As for the male voters, I hired a company that had a very sophisticated phone system. An operator would call voters and say, "Would you be willing to listen to a very short message from Susan Guber, a candidate for the Florida Senate in your area?" Unbelievably, very few people said no. The operator would push a button which played a short tape that I had recorded. I kept the tape to thirty seconds. I gave my name, stated that I was a candidate for state representative, and said that I would like their support. I also gave my phone number in case someone wanted to talk to me. Then the operator would thank the person for his time. If the feedback from the voter seemed positive, the operator would mark the list with our grading system (see Chapter 16) so that we could recall these people just before the election. I could not have done this in 1986 because the technology was not available. If you are running in a primary, your party can give you the names of companies that have information, technology, or services that may be helpful. There is also a government publication called *Campaigns and Elections,* which comes out every other month. It keeps up with the latest devices available for candidates. (Contact Joseph Griggs at 212-563-3851.) Another resource is the yellow pages in your phone book, where there are listings for phone services, mail services, and temporary office workers.

We were able to collect enough money to hire temps to fill in on the phone bank, for poll watching on the day of the election, and for rides to the polls. Anything that accomplishes the task of getting to the voter on your behalf is a good idea, because you can't possibly cover a large voting district yourself.

Call other candidates in your area to find out about new ideas and services. I found that waiting time at a candidates' forum was a great opportunity to network with other candidates who were not running in my race. Some have great ideas and are very resourceful. Vendors to candidates seem to come out of nowhere once you file for office.

One word of caution: Not all ideas are good ones, and you have to use technology wisely. One opponent in the 1988 Democratic primary had so much money that he had a video made, complete with scenes of him bashing me. He paid to have copies of the video hand delivered to all Democrats in the district. Each tape was packaged in an unmarked box labeled "important message enclosed." Many voters were irate because they felt they had been hoodwinked into watching a political advertisement. Moreover, they felt that the candidate was wasting money, something they did not want their elected official to do. I received many calls from voters who said that they would never vote for someone who wasted money like that. Another lesson is that if you run against an incumbent, you must establish yourself as a worthy candidate before you trash your opponent. Be judicious in what methods you select and use common sense—that never fails in any race.

■ **New technological advances are developing rapidly. Find out what is available and use it judiciously.**

13

Using Signs

A political campaign sign can be anything from a billboard to a handout taped to a wall. In my campaign, we used four kinds of signs: (1) bus bench signs, (2) signs to be displayed in store windows, (3) literature used as door hangers, and (4) bumper stickers. These were adequate for a state representative race. We began by buying the bus bench signs six months before the election. That gave us enough time to secure the best locations. Prices are the same regardless of the location, and I got a package deal of ten signs for $3,000, including the cost of the artwork and production; however, prices change and vary from city to city. Candidates are usually asked to pay up front, so having money in your bank account is important. It is also important to check out the election laws, because you may have to include your party affiliation and a disclaimer (i.e., paid political ad) on the signs.

One Sunday morning, when there was little traffic, my husband and I rode along the main streets in the district. Michael took the wheel while I took a pad of paper. As we drove, I noted the locations of all the best signs, the ones on the main arteries, and those that could be seen from an intersection. I also made a list of first and second choices in case a location was under contract and not available.

When we put our signs up, many people thought we had dozens of signs. The high visibility of our signs made it look like they were everywhere. This really "kicked off" the campaign. We chose red and white for our colors, which stood out among all the green in Florida. The signs simply said "Guber." If you looked closely, they also said "Susan for..." and "State Representative District 117." I also included the name of my campaign treasurer in small print, as he was well known. Weeks before the other candidates had any signs around, these ten signs were working their magic. People began wondering who "Guber" was, and that in itself was a "good sign."

A month later, I bought small signs printed with my picture for store windows. Every weekday morning for two weeks, I took the signs and my literature to the stores around the district. I asked each proprietor whether I could post my sign in his or her window. About one in ten stores allowed me to put a sign up. I always carried my own masking tape and made sure I took the store owner's business card back to headquarters. When I returned, I sent a letter of thanks and kept a list of locations for future campaigns. Some owners were short of window space but nonetheless allowed me to affix my campaign literature to the door. I found that the chain stores and gas stations did not allow signs, but there were always exceptions, especially if I was a valued customer.

A man who was interested in my campaign asked me if my headquarters was being housed in "Mario's," a tailor/dry-cleaning establishment. It seemed that Mario was such a good supporter that he had my signs all over his store. If anyone casually drove by, it looked as if my campaign was based there. From the amount of business our family gave him, he must have felt we deserved the visibility.

Your background can bring constituencies to help you. Think about who you can contact. By being a little creative, you'll be able to enlist the help of others. For example, if you are in a profession such as teaching, law, real estate, or insurance, talk to colleagues about providing assistance. Friends from church, PTA, or charity groups are good contacts; find a way to mobilize them all. I had a friend who was a lobbyist for the railroad workers. He wanted to help mornings and suggested his men could do any heavy physical work. We put their strength to good use angling the concrete bus benches for better visibility.

I had worked for the local hospital association, and some of my best contacts came through the hospitals and the physicians in the community. My husband, who is a physician, spread the word to his friends that I was running. He put signs and literature in the five doctors' lounges of the hospitals where he worked. The doctors needed help with state laws regarding malpractice insurance and were only too glad to get involved. I also knew that doctors have patients from all over the district who come to their offices. People ranging in age from teens to the elderly sit in their waiting rooms. In May, I began paying morning visits to every physician's office in the area. Many locate their offices in medical office buildings, so it is easy to visit many doctors' offices at once. If the doctor was busy, I asked the staff if I could tape a small campaign card to the sliding glass reception window. Many allowed it. Others had to check with their boss, but I kept a list and called to follow up. Many voters who visited their doctor's office during the campaign told me they had seen my sign in the waiting room. If I saw the physician, I would leave a bumper sticker. I also left literature in the waiting room and a contribution envelope with the receptionist. Once again, I made it easy for the office by bringing my own supplies. Leaving signs for others to post won't do. People with the best of intentions forget. One morning as I was doing my "rounds," a young doctor said,

"I've heard of you" and proceeded to write a nice check. I received several contributions in this way. Venturing out into these offices helped spread the word, and the signs spread it even further. By going store to store, I met the personnel and storekeepers in the same manner. Get out into the community as much as you can. I have seen candidates spend valuable time sitting around their head-quarters "brainstorming" with their staff. It's meeting with citizens around town that wins votes.

Campaigns, as a rule, take place during the warm weather months. Across the country right before an election, you'll see candidates at busy intersections holding signs. While it may not seem like a very dignified activity, it nonetheless gets attention. I certainly couldn't pass up this free opportunity for visibility. Furthermore, I wanted to make my sign-holding routine unique. A lawyer friend came up with the idea of using the old Burma Shave technique, which is basically a series of signs that form a message. Another friend thought we should use "If You Knew Susie" as a slogan. We combined the two ideas and had four large signs hand painted, each with one word on it. I held the "Susie" sign. My volunteer coordinator enlisted three sign-holders to appear with me. We stood at busy intersections and spaced ourselves so that people could read the message while driving by. We did this during rush hour for a week prior to the election. We did it mornings and evenings and in different locations. No one knew where we would pop up.

The media called and wanted to know where we would be located next. We were lucky because the television stations and local papers publicized our sign-holding project in the news. Free publicity is wonderful in a campaign. Again, try to be creative. You could even wind up on television.

People in their cars had various reactions. Most thought it was cute or funny and would indulge us with a smile. Some gave us the "thumbs up" sign, and some

VOTE FOR
EXPERIENCE
SEPT. 2

Susan
GUBER
*"BEST QUALIFIED
BY FAR"*

Bulk Rate
U.S. Postage
PAID
Miami, Florida
Permit No. 1444

If you knew Susie...

For Absentee Ballot, call 375-5858

Candidate's sign

even a honk. As people stopped for a traffic light, they would try to chat with us. Before the first primary, one man pulled over and said that he was a friend of one of my opponents, but if I defeated him, he would help us because of the work I had done in the community and the great campaign we were waging. Years later, people remind me of those signs and how effective they were. It may sound foolish to stand around in traffic, and you certainly shouldn't do anything that makes you uncomfortable, but you also shouldn't turn down a good opportunity to make an impact on the voters.

Budd Gardner, a state senator, was the victim of some mischief one day as he stood on a bridge waving to passing cars. He was "mooned" by a passenger. I don't know if that meant he was against Bud's candidacy or all candidates, but it indeed proves that anything can happen. Have a sense of humor; it helps immeasurably.

A word of caution about what is acceptable in different districts: Some communities have no qualms about campaign signs hanging from sides of buildings, displayed on roofs, nailed to trees, or erected on front lawns. Certain municipalities even expect the use of signs mounted on wooden boards almost the size of billboards. My district tended to be conservative, environmentally conscious, and suburban. I personally dislike billboards and large campaign signs. There is also the problem of taking signs down after the election. Indeed, many communities have laws governing the size of signs and how long after the election they can remain standing. There can be heavy fines for each day after an election that the signs remain. Learn your local laws, and make sure your staff and volunteers know them as well. Remember that you are responsible for everything having to do with your campaign, even overzealous assistants who may not know how to comply with local ordinances.

Because of the type of district I was hoping to represent, I kept my signs to bus benches and store windows. Thus, I didn't have to worry about offending anyone or how to dispose of the signs. It's only natural to become concerned when you see hundreds or even thousands of billboards and signs for your opponent posted around town. Stick to your plan, whatever it is, and remember: Signs don't vote!

- **Decide on the types of signs you want to use.**

- **Plan to install signs in strategic places.**

- **Use discretion and taste in choosing placement of signs.**

- **Plan to remove signs after the election.**

14

Using Mail and
the Media

With my publicist, Dick Rundell, I developed a
master plan and time line for sending mail and
buying advertising. We sent campaign literature to all the Democrats for the three elections. In the
second and third elections, I sent literature to Republicans as well. (In the first campaign, I was ill advised not
to send mailings to the opposition party. Now I know that
undecided voters will vote for the person and not by party
affiliation. After the general election, we could tell by the
number of votes cast in certain precincts that Republicans did vote for me.)

Mr. Rundell designed oversized postcards to mail to
registered voters. We agreed that people read campaign
literature en route from the mailbox to the trash can, so
we made sure it was easy to read and that there was
nothing to open. The literature bore my name and a large
picture on the address side (see illustration). We used

Oversized postcard

bright colors "to catch the eye" and varied the color of the card for each election. We also sent out a series of four cards for the general election. Each one focused on a hot issue and gave my position on it. We tackled gun control, abortion, drinking laws, and funding for education. I felt strongly about these issues, and people wanted to know where I stood. My opponent had voted for two controversial bills, one having to do with carrying a concealed weapon and the other dealing with the reproductive rights of women. Rundell advised that we create a caricature of my opponent depicting his stand on these issues. As soon as the cartoon was sent to the voters, the newspaper called and wanted to do a story about it, which gave us additional publicity. Using a cartoon or some other eye-catching idea will get the voters' attention. People receive lots of junk mail, so your mailings have to be unique.

We also designed a regular size postcard that was printed with a message from a supporter to his or her friends. It told about my candidacy and why the supporter was voting for me. We left room for the supporter's signature. The cards were purchased from the post office and had first-class postage printed on them. The supporter addressed the cards and brought them back to us so that we could mail them. We kept a list of supporters who had taken cards in case we had to remind them of their commitment. Again, we tried to keep control of all the activities having to do with the campaign.

Many candidates send computerized personalized letters. This has become so commonplace that I am not sure it is still successful. The letters can be expensive to produce and look like an advertisement for a contest.

Elect Susan GUBER

STATE REPRESENTATIVE
DISTRICT 117
DEMOCRAT

Dear

I am writing you on behalf of Susan Guber, a Democratic candidate for State House District 117. There are a number of candidates on the ballot, but none as qualified, informed and sincere as Susan. She has an excellent background in government and civic work. As a former public school teacher, she places high priority on improvements in public education. Her years of involvement and knowledge of all the issues makes her the best choice for State Representative in District 117. Please join with me in voting for Susan Guber on September 2nd.

J.M.A. endorsed

Sincerely,

Linda & Bill Smoak

Pd. Pol. Adv. ■◄■►■

Postcard from supporter

Unless you already know the candidate, I'm not sure you would bother to open it. Years ago, when the technique was new, I recommended it, but today I would go back to using the oversize colorful postcard.

The absentee voter is a very important one to court. Elections have been won by receiving a majority of the absentee vote. A person who takes the time to apply for an absentee ballot will vote! The elections department can supply you with an updated list of voters who have applied for an absentee ballot. People apply daily, right up until the election. Each week, as the department received its requests, we would buy the list of names printed out on mailing labels. We sent the voters a piece of campaign literature along with a hand-written greeting in red ink from me. I tried to write a personal sentence on each card. For example, if a voter was spending the summer in New England, I would mention that I was from there. We even sent a message to absentee voters living abroad.

A terrific service to provide voters, if you have the money, is to send a postcard telling them how to register as an absentee voter. The voter simply indicates that he or she wants an absentee ballot and drops the card in a mailbox *mailed back to you!* You keep a copy of the cards on which voters request an absentee ballot so that you can send them your literature and have the elections department mail them the absentee ballot. This is one way of showing how you can be helpful to your constituents. Check with your elections department to find out how you must word your postcard for proper processing of absentee ballots.

In order to mail to thousands of voters, you will need to purchase a bulk mail permit at your central post office. Bulk mail (or direct mail as it is sometimes called) saves you a tremendous amount of money. It is worthwhile to take the time to learn how to prepare bulk mailings. I recommend all large mailings be done by a professional mail company. You can prepare small contributor or ab-

---

ABSENTEE BALLOT REQUEST FOR NOVEMBER 8 ELECTION

Name of voter _____

Address of voter _____

City _____ State _____ Zip Code _____

Address where ballot should be mailed _____

Date of Birth _____ Registration Number (if known) _____

Signature _____

Reason for requesting absentee ballot:

_____ Unable to vote without anothers assistance to attend polls
_____ I will not be in County of residence during election hours
_____ I will be an election worker on November 8
_____ Religious tenets

Absentee ballot request

sentee ballot mailings yourself with the help of your volunteers. All the pieces have to be identical mail and bundled together by zip code. Because there were many zip codes in our district, we wound up sorting the letters on the floor in zip code order. The post office will give you instructions and will also tell you the date that your bulk mail needs to be sent. Campaign mail is priority mail the week before an election, and the post office will tag your mail as such. Learn all of the post office rules.

In our area, radio time was not too expensive, so we bought time on stations we thought were popular. Again, a good publicist can advise you. Miami is multicultural and has stations that broadcast in French or Spanish. Decide if you need to appeal to a certain group. It pays to hire a good producer for your radio spots. You will want to come across as sounding very professional. Our sixty-second production used the deep voice of a very authoritative-sounding man.

Newspapers are another medium that should be left to the professional. My publicist wrote clean, clear ads that got the message across succinctly and included pictures and color. Color ads are more expensive, but Mr. Rundell felt that they really are worth the extra money. We began running our ads three weeks before the election and ran a different ad each week. Moreover, we contracted with only the neighborhood section of our paper, which saved money.

The largest portion of our budget was used for direct mail. Some mail went only to women, some to minorities, and others to the whole electorate. Next we budgeted for radio and newspapers. Television is wonderful if you are running in a large area that would be impossible to cover by mail. Most large county or state campaigns depend upon television. It would have been overkill when I ran in a district race; however, when I ran for the state senate (a 300-mile, quarter-of-a-million-voter race), I did use television. Let your publicist make that decision for you. That's why you pay for his or her expertise.

You never know what will and what won't work in a campaign. There is no scientific formula, only good advice. The best publicity is still free positive publicity. You will be interviewed by the local media, and they will give some coverage to the race. However, in a large city, where there are many other candidates and issues, you will not get much exposure. If you get an endorsement from a newspaper, you can use it in your advertisements. I talked with reporters in coffee shops and by phone and answered questionnaires through the mail.

There is no special way to prepare for press interviews. Study the issues and practice answering questions succinctly. Reporters like a concise direct answer. Wait a few seconds before responding to a question. Try to avoid saying your remarks are off the record, because the reporters are trying to write a story. Tell them what you can talk about instead of what you can't. If you do not have an opinion or do not know the answer, tell them that you will get back to them. As with anyone you meet during the campaign, try to remember to get their business card. You can always call the reporter if you want to add something to the interview. Be polite, and if a nice article is printed, call the reporter and thank him or her.

I once asked Dante Facell what the most unusual happening throughout all his campaigns was. He said, "I once had an opponent who refused to talk to the press." This indeed is strange because publicity is so valuable. It has become popular to bash the press, but I have found that 90% of the members do a good job, which is a better record than most professions. If you are candid and forthright, the press will treat you fairly.

- ■ **Hire a good political consultant to help with public relations and the media.**

- ■ **Learn about bulk mail regulations.**

- ■ **Create a plan for mail, radio, newspaper, and television ads.**

15

Creating a Public Image

The rah, rah, hip, hip, hooray part of a campaign is always great fun. Although it is time consuming to get ready for special events, they can pay off in media attention and a change of pace. One example is an idea that Senator Bob Graham of Florida used when he ran for governor of the state. He called it his "work days." He signed up for a different job each month, and the media followed him wherever he went.

Governor Lawton Chiles of Florida tells the following story: "When I announced my plans to run for the United States Senate in 1970, I was a Florida State Senator, known in my immediate district, but not state-wide. I began a walk from Century, Florida, to the Florida Keys, encompassing 1,003 miles. This campaign tactic earned me the name of 'Walking Lawton' and became the center-piece of the campaign. It enabled me to run a campaign that was extremely low-budgeted, plus put me in contact with thousands of individuals that I met along the walk."

Getting out in public at large events provided necessary relief from the tedious, grueling work and kept my
volunteers going. These events require research into the
proper protocol for the occasion. Since I had worked in
the political community before, I pretty much knew what
to expect. For example, I knew that at the three major
political luncheons sponsored by chambers of commerce
and a current events club, it was customary for the candidate to buy tickets for a whole table and have supporters sit with him or her. I also knew that it was sanctioned
to put literature at the other tables and signs around the
room. Other candidates (not knowing this) came alone,
looking like lost sheep. Become familiar with each club's
rules. Call beforehand so that you can do what is customary. It will make you feel confident and part of the
membership.

Author Jeffrey Archer was the youngest member ever
elected to the House of Commons in Great Britain. He
tells of a strategy that brought him recognition at a time
when he was virtually unknown. Mr. Archer had a contact at a daily newspaper whom he would call each day
for a list of events that the paper's photographers would
be covering. He made a point of attending as many of the
functions as possible and made sure he stood as close as
possible to the people being photographed. With luck, his
name would be included along with the photo. It was only
a matter of time before he was recognized throughout his
community.

My own district encompassed a beautiful area called
Key Biscayne. (Former President Nixon had a vacation
compound there, complete with heliport.) Every Fourth of
July, the Key Biscayne Chamber of Commerce puts together a series of events, beginning with a marathon run.
There is a wonderful old-fashioned parade down the main
street of the island, and the whole town turns out. What
an opportunity to see almost every voter and to have
every voter see me! We decided to pay particular attention

to Key Biscayne that weekend and rented three motel rooms on the ocean. One room was for male volunteers, one was for female volunteers, and one was for my husband and myself. We stocked the rooms with snacks and cold drinks. During the three days, forty of our door-to-door volunteers used the rooms to freshen up and relax between walks. They could also use the pool and the beach. It must have been 100 degrees, but no one seemed to mind. We knew that the people living on the key would be home on the Fourth, and we took advantage of it. In the three days we stayed there, we visited every Democrat in every single-family home on the island—more than 1,400 people. The highlight of the festivities was the parade. Many of the candidates rode in convertibles. We didn't have one. Instead, a friend who was a building contractor loaned me his truck. Frank drove it and my daughter, together with her volunteers, decorated it with crepe paper, bunting, and posters. A group of us jumped in the back. I stood on a platform so that I could be a little taller (I am 5'2"). We also heard that it was customary for parade participants to throw candy or little toys to the children along the route. Not to be outdone, we bought (from a wholesale supply company) huge tubs of bubble gum and threw pieces of gum out of the truck to all the kids lining the parade route. People never forgot it; they still tell me how successful our "float" was. Years after I was elected, we continued the tradition, only we changed to a friend's flashy red convertible. The friend is now running for judge.

The Fourth of July and Labor Day are traditional political bonus days. A list of events going on in the community appears in the newspapers. On Labor Day, our congressman would hold an enormous picnic. It was an extravaganza equaled only by a three-ring circus. There were bands, free food, rides for kids, bagpipe players, and of course the congressman. All the local politicians and candidates came to hand out literature. Some wore out-

Fourth of July parade

rageous hats or signs. We brought our road signs with the words "If You Knew Susie," and four volunteers held the signs aloft in the proper sequence. Then we got lucky. Because these signs were so large, bright, and different, the television stations zeroed in on them. We appeared on the six and eleven o'clock news programs on all three local television channels. Nothing in the world is better for a candidate than free television time.

These events take time and lots of thought to plan. It took Elizabeth many hours to organize the Key Biscayne weekend. In addition, she had to be on hand to make sure the volunteers knew what to do when they arrived. She had to reserve the motel rooms well in advance, buy the snacks and decorations, and line up the many volunteers. Starting your campaign early in the election cycle and having money in your campaign account helps when you need it the most.

My appearance was an important aspect of creating a public image. The expression "dress for success" was meant for candidates. Never again will you be seen by so many people. First impressions are important. People will silently scrutinize and judge you based on your grooming and clothes. One friend of mine even had a tummy tuck before he ran for a higher office. That may be a bit drastic, but the point is you should try to look your best. There were eight candidates in our primary. All were qualified and most appeared well turned out. Make sure you look like you fit into the community. Unfortunately, it may be the only way some people will judge your candidacy.

I decided that I would use red and white as my campaign colors. White is a great contrast with any color, and by using only one other color, we kept costs down. I chose a color that would look good on me. I wore a red dress whenever I could and used the color on all printed materials. If you are unsure of your appearance, do not hesitate to get some professional advice from a consultant to spruce up your image.

I have been told that certain colors will wake audiences up, while others put them to sleep. Wear a bright necktie or suit. In addition to being neat and wearing a bright article of clothing, appropriateness to the occasion is critical. I have seen candidates in soiled clothes and women with long red fingernails and stiletto heels. Very trendy clothes or non-business dress is self-defeating. Remember, you will be representing the people. The candidate who makes the best first impression doesn't look much different from the businessperson on the street. One woman whose campaign color was yellow bought five different yellow dresses and always looked great during her campaign.

Dressing professionally in 110-degree weather is not easy. I wore white cotton dresses (to stay cool) in parades and picnics, along with my red name tag. Walking door to door was easiest for me in Bermuda shorts and a polo shirt. The most important item, however, was a pair of good quality walking shoes or hiking boots. Many times I could have walked into fire ants or even a snake, and I was glad to have been wearing socks and sturdy shoes.

Meetings demand strictly business attire, and all of the credible candidates are dressed in this manner. However, some nights, after a door-to-door walk, I would stop by a candidates' forum dressed in my Bermuda shorts. I had to make a decision as to which took precedence if there was no time to change.

On one occasion at the Fourth of July parade, I noticed a candidate dressed in a blazer, tie, and long pants. It was so hot I thought he would pass out. He never took off the jacket. I have also seen men in three-piece suits and women in high heels at picnics, and they looked out of place. One woman who wore high heels to a picnic sank into the soft ground, looking rather tipsy. You need to be comfortable on the trail; there is no reason to suffer.

On some days, I changed my clothes several times. I started out at a chamber of commerce breakfast dressed in a suit. Then I changed to a skirt, short-sleeved blouse, and flat shoes to carry my posters store to store. I changed back to the suit for a luncheon and later put on shorts to canvass neighborhoods. After dinner, I put the suit back on to go to a candidates' forum. I expended more energy changing clothes than anything else that day. That was why it was terrific having the campaign headquarters in my house. I saved time by not having to cart clothes around. If you keep a raincoat, umbrella, extra shoes, and a sweater in your car, you will be ready for all types of weather conditions.

One last word about clothes. One friend showed up to canvas homes in a linen dress and high heels. We had failed to tell her how to dress. We did not waste her time however; she was the driver that day for the person who actually went to each door. Make sure your volunteers know what they will be doing and what to wear when you sign them up.

I even managed to walk on most rainy days. With a poncho, red of course, and an umbrella to keep the literature dry, I was in business.

Former State Representative Betty Metcalf broke her foot on a curb during her third bid for re-election, even though she was wearing walking shoes. She never gave up her door-to door activities though; she had a friend wheel her around in a wheelchair and kept on going. She received lots of press coverage and managed to win with 70% of the vote!

Each night after the campaign staff left the house, I would review the next day's activities and plan what to wear. That way, I was prepared and did not have to decide what to wear at the last minute. Good planning is the name of the campaign game.

- ■ Research the customs for the events you will be attending.

- ■ Dress neatly, comfortably, and appropriately for all occasions.

- ■ Pick a complimentary color for your theme; wear it, and use it for signs, literature, and ads.

16

Dealing with Candidates' Forums and Dealing with Opponents

About six months before my first primary, I became heavily involved in candidates' forums. There were eight people in the race, and it seemed that every group imaginable wanted to see the contestants. The groups ranged from the Rotary Club to the League of Women Voters. Some clubs videotaped us as we were paraded through, asked to speak, and questioned.

Whether or not to participate in a forum is a valid question. In my first race, all the candidates were new to politics, and I felt that I had to participate. However, if you think that a particular club is biased, do not agree to debate. Even in my last race, which was for the Florida Senate, I was still somewhat naive. I agreed to go to a black church where my black opponent was being supported openly by the pastor. I did not know this for sure, but it was a good bet. I felt that I could represent the people as well as he and thought I could convince the people to vote for the best person. Much to my embarrassment, I received a public lecture about "taking away a black seat." In 1990, reapportionment laws were passed by Congress to maximize minority seats. In the South, it meant gerrymandering districts to ensure more minorities would be elected.

If you feel that you are being "set up," there is no reason to put yourself through this ordeal, because you will not gain anything. This kind of debate is not a debate at all.

My friend Katy Sorenson, who was elected to the county commission, ran against an effective incumbent and a strong debater who had been in politics for many years. He not only was an attorney, but his depth of knowledge on the issues was vast. However, the incumbent had a fatal flaw. Allegations of sexual harassment and ethics violations filled the newspaper daily. The *Miami Herald* ran unfavorable articles detailing his escapades. One headline read "Hawkins' Office Was a Hellhole." Of course, Mr. Hawkins denied the allegations, but the *New Times Miami* paper said, "The more Hawkins denied the allegations, the guiltier he appeared. When an investigator from the Florida Commission on Ethics asked him if he repeatedly knocked a bullet off his desk so he could look down the blouse of his secretary when she picked it up—as the secretary had alleged—he responded with this: 'There wasn't anything down her blouse. She's a very small-chested woman. It doesn't take a genius to figure that out.' And when an employee of Vietnam Veterans of America accused the commissioner of exposing himself to her and trying to fondle her breasts, Hawkins, who served on the organization's board of directors, said that the charge was ludicrous because he is only attracted to good-looking women."

Before Katy decided to run, we talked about her chances of winning against a well-known incumbent with a bankroll of $250,000, which grew to $550,000. I said that the media would help her by running negative articles but told her she would have to keep up the negative pressure. Too often, candidates, especially women, hesitate to run a negative campaign. In this instance, there was every reason to talk about the incumbent's lapse in ethics. The public needed to know in order to choose between a newcomer with no experience and a candidate with fifteen years under his belt. Lack of trust is a very powerful weapon, and this was truly a campaign issue. Ms. Sorenson did get into the race as the only woman in a field of nine candidates. She did her homework and won with a two to one vote over the incumbent in the primary. She raised money, walked door to door, and had a very effective phone bank.

She ran against the incumbent in the general election and was asked to participate in many debates. A couple of phony groups were hastily put together by the opponent. She wisely refused to appear. However, she did appear at legitimate debates. I'm not sure she needed to debate her opponent at all, but she felt pressured and agreed to appear. Debates tend to attract people whose minds are already made up, so there is little to gain in the way of votes. The audience is usually made up of friends of one of the candidates. Besides, her opponent knew the issues very well. I believe that her time would have been better spent on grass-roots campaigning rather than making so many public appearances which could only call attention to her lack of knowledge on the issues. However, after some difficult episodes toward the end of the campaign, Katy became pretty savvy. She would tell the audience, "I may not have the depth of knowledge that my opponent has, but I do know the difference between right and wrong." This line made a great sound bite for the media, and she began to hit her opponent again and again on the ethics charges. She cleverly never mentioned the phrase "sexual harassment," which is a turnoff to men; instead, she talked about his ethical short-comings. This cleverly gave her the edge in a difficult situation.

If you do agree to debate, and you believe there will be a level playing field, remember to tailor your remarks to your audience. No single opening statement will suffice for all forums. For example, James Lombard, former state representative from Osprey, Florida, tells of an opponent who blew his chances for election at a forum. "On the Saturday prior to Election Day, I met my opponent for the first time on the campaign trail. We spoke, along with the other office-seekers, in a candidates' forum at a mobile home park. My talk focused on the broad constitutional issues on the following Tuesday's ballot. The other fellow made an elaborate presentation of his views on United States foreign policy versus that of totalitarian nations! The final vote in that precinct was 2,129 to 1 in my favor."

By the same token, many Cuban-American candidates in sections of Dade County, which is heavily Hispanic, open their remarks by ripping Fidel Castro apart. Running for a county or state office has nothing to do with Castro, but the audience loves this subject, and many a Cuban candidate has been elected by voicing his or her wrath about the dictatorship in Cuba. Know your audience, and try to say something that makes them feel you understand them and are one of them.

When I first began going to candidates' debates and forums, I was extremely nervous. I knew I was being compared to my opponents, and indeed I was! I tried to wear something bright, like a red dress, so I would stand out. Excellent grooming and a neat appearance not only help you look good but increase your confidence. Being the only woman in the race helped me, too.

I found all of the candidates in my race to be friendly, and we would joke together: "It must be Wednesday, it's the Chamber of Commerce Forum." We developed a camaraderie by going through an ordeal together. It reminded me of other times in my life when friendships developed out of being in the same situation with others. When my husband, Michael, was in medical school and my children were babies, I developed a closeness with the other young students' wives. When Michael was in Vietnam, it was commiseration with other military wives. Even during pregnancy, a closeness develops with other expectant women; the closer you are to your due date, the stronger the bond. The same is true for candidates in an election period. As we sat on the dais, ready to speak, we would whisper among ourselves. Our spouses sat in the audience, cheering us on. Our campaign staff talked with their counterparts. It was a unique experience, and it drew us together. It even became fun. Considering how often I saw my opponents, it was a good idea to befriend them.

I didn't realize that these friendships would pay off later. When I won my first primary, some of my opponents helped me win the second primary. One candidate asked his friends to vote for me, and another candidate's friends walked homes for me and helped raise money. A third opponent was a long-time friend. Our daughters had been friends since first grade and were now college graduates. They were working on our respective campaigns and hadn't seen each other in many years. At a luncheon for the candidates, the girls not only were delighted to see each other but made plans to get together after work. I never had any hostility toward my opponents. After the runoff election, all of the Democrats helped me in the race against the Republican candidate.

I have always felt that it is easier to go through life being a friend. I can't imagine meeting a former opponent and not greeting him or her. Having a sense of humor and putting the whole campaign in the right perspective made my life easier. A political campaign takes up only a small portion of one's life. I intend to live in my community for many years, with my opponents as neighbors. I look back on my campaigning days as fun.

Another trick I learned was not to dwell on or worry about what my opponents were doing. It is a waste of time. If you are well organized and work according to a timetable, there is nothing more you can do. If I had gotten caught up in what the other seven candidates were up to, I would not have had time to run my own campaign. One woman who ran for the Florida House spent half her time getting up in the middle of the night and tearing her opponent's signs down. Needless to say, she lost, and with such a limited strategy and destructive attitude, she deserved to lose.

Legislator Jack Ascherl, from New Smyrna Beach, Florida, tells a story about becoming paranoid during his campaign:

> A rustic country dweller complained to me that someone in the opponent's camp had dumped about 300 of my campaign signs on his property, rather than taking them to the dump. (He thought the election was over, but there were still two weeks to go.) That night a good friend and I lay hidden in the woods with a camera until 4:00 a.m., hoping to catch my opponent in the act of dumping signs, but he didn't show. Nevertheless, I have great pictures in my election scrapbook of ourselves and some poor hunter we scared half to death early in the morning.

How to Handle Questions from the Audience

When it came time to answer questions, it turned out they were easier than I had imagined. Because the issues don't change, the questions are always the same. After days of answering the same questions over and over again, I got my answers down pat. If I was asked a question I didn't know how to answer, I apologized and said so. If people argued with me or became disagreeable, I would smile, compose myself, and tell them I didn't agree but respected their opinion. Studies have shown that 86% of the impression one makes is based on appearance. Certainly how one handles a disagreeable citizen is more important in terms of appearance than the actual words that are said. By keeping cool, you will win the hearts of the voters watching the process with your composed handling of the situation.

Former Congressman Bill Lehman tells of the most burning issue in his 1972 race: "It was court-ordered busing for the purpose of racial integration. All of the conventional wisdom said that to have any chance of winning, a candidate should support a constitutional amendment prohibiting forced busing. I was the only candidate in a field of ten who opposed vocally an anti-busing constitutional amendment." Mr. Lehman served in Congress for over thirty years. Being honest about your position helps. It is much easier through the years to remember how you stand on an issue if you are consistent and honest about your feelings. If you think the district wants you to support something, but in your heart you know it is wrong, stick with what you believe is right.

On the other hand, if new information changes your position on an issue, do not be inflexible. As long as you can justify your change of mind, voters understand; indeed, some are even more supportive because it shows you can be open to new ideas and are human.

The candidates' forums are not as important in the grand scheme of a grass-root campaign as you might imagine. The door-to-door effort gave me much better access to voters. It was my highest priority, considering the time I devoted to it versus other parts of the campaign. I felt so strongly about this that many times I would be out walking in casual attire and would have to attend a forum just as I was dressed.

As time went on, I became less and less nervous about the forums. I even started to enjoy them when summer arrived. They meant I could get out of the heat for a spell.

Ron Saunders, who ran for Florida secretary of state, tells of when he first ran for the House from a large district which included all of the Florida Keys. "I had attended every campaign event, but one night I had several to attend. I stayed to speak at one rally and then jumped in my car to reach the other rally, which was twenty-five miles away. Since the debate was being broadcast on the radio, I could hear each candidate speak until I got there. I arrived in the parking lot in a cloud of dust just as my opponent finished speaking, much to her chagrin and to the surprised relief of my supporters." The fact that the debate was broadcast on the radio increased Ron's exposure, and he was able to hear what was being said before he got there. The talk in the community about the debate and the media coverage, if there is any, are the most important parts of any political debate.

- Try to maintain a friendly relationship with your opponent.

- Debate your opponent if you believe the forum will benefit your campaign.

- Don't worry about the other races. Channel all your energy into your own campaign.

- Negative campaigning can be useful if done with discretion and honesty.

17

Walking Door to Door

A long-time member of the Florida House of Representatives, Sam Mitchell of Chipley, Florida, told
me, "Rural areas have very personable people and
nothing takes the place of person-to-person contact in an
election campaign in my district. At almost every cross-
road, we have a political gathering. Entertainment would
include music and plenty of fresh mullet. This kind of
process really brings out my constituents for the ol' fash-
ion' handshake. They like it and I love it!"

Sam's victory may have been attributed to a series of
fish fries, but if I could attribute my victory to any one
aspect of campaigning, it would be walking door to door.
That meant going to each house in the district, ringing
the doorbell, introducing myself, and leaving a piece of
campaign literature. It may sound simple, but it is a
complicated, time-consuming, and exhausting process. It
is also crucial. If there is a secret to winning—some magic
charm—that is it. This technique is feasible in district
elections, but in large county or statewide districts, you
have to pick perhaps a few key areas and hope the word
spreads. In districts that are made up of many condos or

apartments, try to have a leader of the condo association host an event where you can meet the voters in each building.

Congressman Dick Gephardt of Missouri, together with his wife and mother-in-law, knocked on 50,000 doors in his district to win his first election. The late Congressman Claude Pepper said, "Nothing can be more effective than the hard work in a political campaign of walking to a voter's door."

How to Begin

Before I ever stepped out of my house, I did some "legwork." I began by calling upon a member of the legislature during one of her re-election campaigns and accompanied her when she went door to door. She advised me on how a candidate decides where to begin walking and what to bring on the walks. It seems she began with her own precinct and worked in concentric circles away from her home. That made sense, because I knew my neighbors well and had been involved in the community. Psychologically, it gave me a boost, because the response from my neighbors was positive.

Then there were materials I had to prepare. The elections department supplied us with a list of the voters in each precinct. If money is tight, you can buy a few precinct lists at a time. As soon as you open your bank account and sign up with the elections department to become a candidate, you are eligible to buy voter lists and information. In order to get a list, we had to send a check to the elections department, wait for the list to be processed, and then send someone to pick it up. Having a "runner" helps avoid wearing yourself out.

To begin in the Democratic primary, I needed only the Democratic voter list. In Florida, you cannot vote in a primary for anyone but a candidate from your party. If you are an independent, you cannot vote in a primary. Find out who votes in primaries in your state and target just those voters. The elections department also supplied us with a list of voters who had actually voted in the last primary. That cut down the number of people for the walks. The voter lists can be prepared in many ways: in street order, alphabetical order, precinct order, or zip code order. For walks, you want a list of voters by party affiliation, who votes in certain elections, by precinct, and in street or address order. This organizes the task and makes it quite manageable. We took the list of voters and gave each walker thirty names and addresses of voters, along with a map of those streets. Since the list was arranged by street address, the walker could go up one street and down the next looking for the number of the home he or she wanted to visit. We also marked the streets on an enlarged map with a highlighter.

We then assembled a volunteer kit which included the voter list, map, literature, bumper stickers, a pencil, and Post-It notepads stamped "Sorry I missed you, Susie" (see illustration). A Post-It was applied to the literature if a voter was not home. The kits were simply red paper folders, like schoolchildren use.

The Walk

Each walk covered thirty or fewer homes, depending upon how difficult the homes were to find and how far apart they were. The volunteers met at headquarters, where Elizabeth greeted them and gave them a kit and a campaign badge. It was important that they wore identification so that voters would not be afraid to open their doors. We divided the volunteers into teams of two. One person drove and one walked. Each team was supplied with water and bug repellent. We made sure the volunteers knew where the area was so they wouldn't get lost.

Door-hanger literature

In the beginning, most of the volunteers had never been involved in this kind of activity, so we always had one of the staff go with a new canvasser. Once a volunteer felt comfortable with the process, he or she was able to accompany a beginner on the next walk. Many of our volunteers became "regulars." One lady, whom I had met at Common Cause meetings, worked at the library and came twice a week for six months! Another volunteered every Sunday and Tuesday for the duration of the entire campaign. One young woman had so much fun that she came into the legislative office to help with constituent casework after the election was over. If you can keep your volunteers happy on their rounds, by not piling on too much work, many of them will come back.

Using the map, the duo located their assigned street and drove to the first home. We had numbered the list so that the walker knew the proper sequence in which to walk. As the walker left the car, the driver would read the name of the person in that house so the walker knew whom to ask for. It is important to use the voter's name. If a person had moved, we did not spend time on that house. We found that new residents are not registered. If there is a "for sale" sign out front, the people are not going to bother to vote. If someone other than the voter answers the door, it is better to ask for the voter. Family members who are not voters do not relay messages. You are wasting your words; just leave the literature. Also, it is important for the walker not to use his or her name; it only confuses the voter. The walker should just say, "I am here for (name candidate) and I'm hoping you will be sure to vote on (date of the election)." Keep your message very short. You do not want to bore or bother the voter, and you need to move on to the next house. Most people just take the literature. If someone does ask a question, the walker should take their phone number and have the candidate call the person back. We were asked very few questions, which amazed me.

Sometimes very enthusiastic voters would offer to help. We gave them a bumper sticker and our phone number. Many people said, "Put the sticker on my car." It was fun to see cars all over town with my name. Bumper stickers were also enclosed in all the thank-you letters to contributors.

At the conclusion of the visit, the volunteer handed the voter my literature and thanked the person for his or her time. If a resident wasn't home, we left a "door-hanger" piece of literature on the doorknob with a Post-It attached. All literature included our phone number in case a voter wanted to call. The door-hanger literature had a hole the size of a doorknob cut out at the top. By law, you must not leave anything in a mailbox.

When the walker returned to the car, he or she ranked the voter's response on the elections department printout as follows:

A   Very positive. A for-sure vote.

B   Friendly but no commitment.

C   Little emotion. The voter took the literature. (Most voters were in this category.)

F   The voter expressed support for an opponent. (This rarely happened because most of the candidates were unknown.)

NH   Not home.

We also noted any items of particular interest. If the voter was a teacher or expressed an interest in an issue, we jotted it down. If there was an impediment such as a high wall or big dog, we noted it as well. We used this information in the phone bank.

During our six months of walks, we had some interesting responses. One Sunday, I was walking in a heavily wooded area and rang a doorbell. "Who is it?" I heard a man ask. I answered, "Susan Guber." Again, "Who is it?" I answered again, only louder. The third time the man asked, I figured he was deaf, so I screamed my name at the door. Then the door opened and there stood a young man, out of breath from running down the stairs. Behind him was a parrot, which said "Who is it?" I felt like an idiot shrieking my name repeatedly to a bird!

In *Living a Political Life*, Governor Madeleine Kunin writes about her first race in 1972. She says that she

> ...was so driven that I was afraid to stop campaigning. After swallowing my last bite of supper, I would get up from the table, kiss the children, tell my husband I'd do the dishes later, get in my car, pick up a friend to join me, and walk door to door....My goal was to connect with these strangers on the other side of the threshold as they eyed me and I eyed them...Could I make the proper impression, so that grasp, to be meaningful, must be flesh to flesh. I marvel now to think how much meaning I placed on each handshake, believing something like a blood transfusion occurred. I felt I was extending life to old people, adult approval to children, and during a few grandiose moments I thought my hand shake was a gift. Still there were awkward moments when I extended my hand, and no one took it. Had anyone seen my arm jut straight out, cut down by rejection, like a fallen limb?...The calloused hand, the firm grasp, the blue veins, all held messages I absorbed through my skin. I gathered visceral knowledge. That brief touch linked me, as in a square dance do-si-do, with a circle of people I would have never encountered had I stayed home, looking at my manicured hands.

Governor Kunin articulates beautifully the emotional side of the door-to-door effort.

Sometimes going to a stranger's door can be downright dangerous. As State Senator Sherman Winn told me, "One of the funniest and scariest moments on the campaign trail happened when my son and I were knocking on doors. I knocked on the door, and a man came out with a shotgun and his dog, telling us to get the hell off his property. As soon as we saw the gun and the dog, we turned around and ran not taking the time to open the gate, but rather we jumped over, running as fast as we could."

Ron Glickman from Tampa said, "I came upon a house which had its front door in its carport. I went up to the front door which was open and rang the bell. Up to that time I had not noticed any signs of the presence of dogs at the residence. When the bell rang two big German shepherds came bounding out the front door. I never turn my back to dogs, so I beat a hasty retreat backpedaling down the carport. The only thing which separated me from the dogs was my rolled-up precinct list. One of the dogs was not too pleased by this impediment and took a bite out of it. However, before the dog devoured the list and got to me, his owner came out to restrain him."

Dogs are not the only hazard, as Bert Harris of Lake Placid, Florida found out: "I was standing at a front door of a home so far in the woods that it is hard to describe, when all of a sudden, I looked up and a rooster came around the corner of the house attacking me with his spurs...I decided I could talk to that family by phone."

Mike Abrams, from North Dade County, went to the door of his college landlady. She said that despite his lousy housekeeping in his college days, she would still vote for him!

I remember walking to a young man's house one rainy Saturday afternoon. He asked me in and gave me a check for $100. He said that he couldn't believe that I was walking on such a bad day. Door-to door canvassing in the rain pays off!

Hurley Rudd, former mayor of Tallahassee, tells of a hot day's campaigning in the South in July: "The front of my trousers became soaked on one hot Saturday morning from perspiration. One of the elderly people I called on that day looked around to see if anyone was listening and whispered 'Hurley, go home. You've wet your pants.'"

Florida's former lieutenant governor steals the show with a door-to-door story told by his father: "During the campaign, his wife and son were campaigning on opposite sides of the street. They were both wearing 'Elect Bobby Brantley' buttons. Upon knocking on a door, Lenny, eight years old, was constantly greeted with 'Oh you must be Bobby Brantley's son!' That evening his mother asked whether he liked campaigning and he replied, 'I like it, but everybody keeps calling me Bobby Brantley's son.' She said to him, 'The next time someone says that to you, tell them you are not Bobby Brantley's son, you are Lenny Brantley.' The next morning sure enough, the first lady who saw him remarked, 'You must be Bobby Brantley's son!' Lenny replied, 'That's not what my mommy says!'"

At the end of the walks, our teams drove back to headquarters. If no one was there, the volunteers dropped off their kit and thermos at my doorstep.

It seems there was forever something on my doorstep. We didn't always have people at headquarters, so it became a joke that my doorstep was an outdoor office. My PR person and volunteers would pick up and drop off materials there. At one point, twenty-two little plastic bags with supplies, each labeled with a volunteer's name, were sitting by the door. They were all picked up when we were out. There is no proper system. Do what ever works for your campaign.

Variations in Walks

There are other methods of door-to-door canvassing. A congressman who represents a district four times as large as mine assembles 100 volunteers on Saturdays and gives them each a precinct and a list. They place the literature in plastic bags and hang it on doors. They don't ring bells, but they go to every house. With a district as large as his, it is the only feasible way to cover the territory.

Another method is to fill a car with people. The driver goes to a precinct, and each person takes a different voter list for a series of streets. Then they all meet the driver at a certain time. This is an ideal method when the homes are close together, but homes were sometimes a half-mile apart in our area, so this method didn't work for me.

Perhaps the most common method is to identify a person who wants to volunteer to be a precinct captain. That person usually lives in the precinct and agrees to run the door-to-door activity and get all of the volunteers. The up side of this method is that you have people who live in the precinct actually working their neighbors, but the down side is that I would have needed thirty-two people, each of whom lived in a different precinct, to come forward to help. We could not replicate this program with our volunteer pool. On two occasions, we had trusted volunteers take care of their own precincts. We knew the volunteers well, and they both came through with flying colors. Each completed the task without our help. All we did was give them the materials. They even ran the phone bank with their volunteers, but you are taking a chance by doing this. I still believe that the best way to canvass is to have complete control over the activities from one centralized location.

Having the walks mapped out by address, with the names of the residents and their party affiliation recorded on paper, was a tremendous advantage. A friend of mine ran in the same district years before and lost. She walked around in business clothes for eight hours a day with no advance organization. She just went house to house with no voter list. She visited everyone—Republicans, Democrats, non-voters, even illegal aliens! She talked to some people for half an hour. At the end of the day, her feet were blistered and bleeding. She did better than I would have expected in the precincts she walked, but she came in next to last out of five candidates. Anticipating, analyzing, and organizing have their merits. Planning my walks and covering the entire district paid off. Out of six contenders in the primary, I got 42% of the vote, a clear majority. I went into the second primary with a distinct advantage; indeed, the election was mine to lose!

Follow Up

Back at headquarters, my daughter and I gathered up the folders, lists, and thermos jugs from the doorstep. The two of us went through the walked lists. Some days, we had a list of 300 people to peruse. First, we removed the names of people who had moved or were supporting an opponent. Then I called people who had a question. There were never many of those. We got their phone numbers by looking them up or buying the list of voter phone numbers. A book called *Bressler's* is available in the library. It lists phone numbers by street address, so that the names on a walk list can be put in street order instead of alphabetical order. This is helpful when you are dealing with location. Thus, we were getting ready daily for our next and last project before the election, the phone bank.

We kept a separate record of people whose numbers were unlisted in the phone book (50% of the numbers are not listed). I sent those people a card reminding them to vote and mentioned that I had visited their home.

I would call the "not at home" people myself after each walk. On rainy nights, it was helpful because I could still stay busy. I would mention that we had walked to the house but no one was there. The best time to call is after dinner, around eight o'clock. I would say, "Mr. Smith? I'm Susan Guber, candidate for the Florida House of Representatives. Last week we came to your house but you were out. We left literature, but I wanted to be able to speak to you personally. I hope you'll remember to vote on November 4." I never asked people to specifically vote for me. I felt it would put them on the spot, and I did not want to get a negative response. I just wanted to get my name out and wanted people to know I cared enough to call. Often they would chat about issues and tell me they were glad I had called. Of course, some people were nicer than others.

One evening after the campaign, I was invited to speak to members of the local Builders' Association. The president came up to me and said, "I was really impressed with your persistence. You not only came to my door, but when I wasn't there you called me. I was out, but my housekeeper gave you my office number. You called me at my office. I'm a life-long Republican, but with that kind of persistence, I sure voted for you!" Once in a while, people were nasty. Some even hung up on me. However, there were many more friendly replies. After each phone call, I evaluated the response and changed the "not home" designation to one of the code letters we had used on the walks. These people were also now ready to be added to the phone bank list.

When we completed walking a precinct, we celebrated by putting a star on that precinct on our huge district wall map. It is amazing how the volunteers watched the map and were thrilled each time a star was added. By the time the primary rolled around, all precincts had stars.

Walks to Apartments and Condominiums

Condos are usually inaccessible for walking door to door, so we looked up the phone numbers of the voters we had targeted and called them. If there are a lot of condos in your district, try to have a condo resident host a breakfast and invite the registered voters. In some areas, the candidate pays for the breakfast and a coordinator who lives in the building makes the arrangements. If you are lucky enough to have such an event donated, so much the better. Be sure that you list the party as an expenditure or an in-kind contribution in your contributor report.

Apartments are a different story, because the residents tend to be somewhat transient. We didn't walk or phone them. Instead, we "blitzed" them with literature just before the election. Our decision to not spend much time walking to each door in an apartment complex was a calculated risk. Studies show that renters vote in very low percentages, whereas homeowners vote in high numbers. Since our district had very few rental properties, we were not risking too many votes.

In my first campaign back in 1986, we kept all of our walk lists on 3″ by 5″ cards, one per home. Today, that data would be kept in a computer. After you have finished walking a precinct, the next step is to delete from your list the names of voters who have moved, whom you have assigned an "F" code on your list, or who are renting. Then make a new list of the precinct in alphabetical order. At this point in the campaign, all you need is the name of the voter or voters in each house, the phone number, and the code designation. (Don't worry about voter address for mailing purposes; a mailing list in zip code order can be purchased from the elections department.) Your new precinct list should contain the following information:

Precinct 100

NAME	CODE	PHONE
Able; Kathy, Robert, Stephen	B	555-4567

By compiling the list after you finish walking each precinct, your phone bank list (see Chapter 23) will be ready at least ten days before the election.

Walking door to door constituted the bulk of our campaign activity. We spent about 70% of our time on this activity. It is a crucial part of the overall scheme. It is very inexpensive, and you can win an election by just having a great door-to door effort. U.S. Congresswoman Carrie Meeks won her first election by walking only in her district and surpassed eight other candidates in votes.

- Buy the selected list of registered voters in your party, arranged in street order.

- Divide the list by precincts and the precincts into manageable walks.

- Have literature and volunteers ready.

- Begin your walks as early in the campaign as possible.

- Keep walks to two hours in duration.

- Follow up by calling those who were not home.

- When you finish walking a precinct, use the data collected to compile a phone bank list.

18

Campaign Ethics

The ethics involved in a campaign essentially are a matter of good taste. How you conduct your campaign will serve as the standard by which you will be perceived in office. The voters have only one criterion by which to judge you as a candidate: your public image. If it is upbeat and positive, then the voters' perception will be positive, too. If, on the other hand, your campaign centers on criticizing your opponent's personal life or flawed character, you will only make yourself look bad. If you are running for an open seat, stress your strong points. If you are running against an incumbent, be careful to stick to the issues and keep personalities out of the race. It is safe to highlight your opponent's voting record, poor attendance, or unethical behavior practices while officially representing the district, but stay clear when the issues delve into a person's personal life. Think through whatever information you impart about your opponent, and be prepared for strong challenge of your remarks. Try not to leave yourself open to criticism. An unscrupulous opponent can slant the truth or even fabricate falsehoods at the last minute to hurt you. A positive approach toward others is well worth fostering.

Grace Cowper, the daughter of the governor of Alaska, told me how her dad ran against a sitting governor who was under impeachment. He used the slogan "Here's straight talk from Steve Cowper." He didn't cite his opponent's troubles; he just ran his campaign according to his own plan. With his positive attitude and the negative press his opponent received, Mr. Cowper won.

Using dirty tricks in a campaign is as old as the campaign process itself. During my first race, two of the six opponents in the primary began attacking each other. Day after day, the paper reported how one was tearing down the other's signs. Of course, the culprit denied any wrongdoing, but one day a volunteer at the offender's headquarters spotted the torn-down signs and took a picture of them. The result was a great story in the paper. We, on the other hand, just continued with our plan of going door to door and did not get involved in these incidents. By staying out of others' campaigns, you will not take valuable time away from the core of the race—getting in touch with voters.

It is important to be courteous to everyone and to be on time. If you attend a campaign forum, it's a good idea to be the first one there. You can meet the audience on a one-to-one basis. People will be impressed that you arrived on time and took the time to spend a few minutes with them.

Also, be extra courteous to your opponents and to their entourage of supporters. The people who support your opponent in one election may be your supporters in the next election. It never pays to make an enemy!

- **Use good taste and the Golden Rule: "Do unto others as you would have others do unto you."**

- **Concern yourself with your own campaign plan instead of your opponent's campaign.**

19

Screening the Candidates

It seems like every special interest group sent me a questionnaire and invited me to an interview with its members. After the interview, they either endorsed my candidacy, opposed it, or sometimes co-endorsed me along with one of my opponents.

These interviews usually follow a prescribed format. Members of the organization's political action committee (PAC) or executive board sit at a long table. You sit on a lone chair or stand at a microphone, facing them. They ask you to tell them a little about yourself and then ask you questions about your campaign and the issues that are important to them. I would give the boundaries of the district and tell them why I was running. When it came time to answer their questions, I found that they usually asked the same questions that were on the questionnaire they had sent. I was always prepared and always did my homework. If I was attending a builders' association screening, I called a builder to discuss builders' issues. If it was the teachers' union, I would find a savvy teacher who was a member of the union. If I found that I disagreed with the organization's philosophy, I would decline to be interviewed. There were two instances when this happened. One was a "Right to Life" group and the other was the National Rifle Association. I disagreed with both groups, and it would have been a waste of my time to obtain their support.

Sometimes your opponent may have an advantage in gaining an endorsement if an influential member of the association goes to bat for him or her. If this happens, go to the interview, do your best, and hope that the group will support you when you win the primary. As always, it pays to be courteous and do your best. I was not endorsed by all the groups that approached me during the campaign. Groups often take opposite sides on issues. The bonus of getting an endorsement lies in the many important resources made available for your campaign. I received PAC money, volunteers, publicity in newsletters, my name in advertisements in the paper listing endorsed candidates, and the best bonus—votes.

One night, we had people from all walks of life at our phone bank, including members of several interest groups. There was a lawyer, doctor, dentist, accountant, carpenter, teacher, builder, banker, and an executive from the local chamber of commerce. The candidate screening had helped supply us with these volunteers. Being endorsed is another avenue for money, publicity, and votes.

Before the first primary, I was not endorsed by one of the local teachers' unions. Being a former teacher, I was devastated. My chief opponent, an architect, had received the endorsement. However, in the general election, I won the endorsement. They must have felt as bad as I during the first round of support, because they went all out to help. They sent a check for $1,000, hosted a fund-raiser, recruited volunteers, and even organized rides to the polls on election day. So carry on and don't be disappointed. There is an old saying in politics: "No permanent friends and no permanent enemies, just permanent issues."

- **Find out the issues that concern a special interest group before you appear at an interview.**

- **Be gracious if a particular group fails to endorse you.**

- **Do not agree to be screened by organizations that you do not support.**

20

Campaigning in the Schools

The mere mention of a political candidate can be a turnoff to some people or groups, and I was sensitive to that. When I tried, for example, to make appearances at Parent-Teacher Association meetings, many times I had to swallow my pride, hoping I would not be turned down or turned away. Other times, it took raw nerve. The reason I targeted schools is I felt that parents involved in PTAs vote.

I had been the chair of an organization called the Citizens' Coalition of Public Schools, a lobby group dedicated to full legislative funding for education. Through the secretary of the organization, I was able to obtain a list of schools and the names and phone numbers of the current PTA presidents. Frank counted thirty-two schools that either were situated in my district or had children from my district attending them. We then began the tedious process of calling to find out when each PTA met. As a former teacher, PTA member, and volunteer in the schools, I felt it was important to attend. PTA meetings in public schools are open to the public; however, they are not used to having an "outsider" attend. The group is usually very small and meets in the morning (a perfect time for a candidate, as there is not much else to do). Sometimes, maybe twice a year, a large group attends and the meeting takes place in the evening. I tried to go to both.

When I was greeted by the president, I would say that I was running for office and wanted to hear about what was currently happening in the school. I always dressed appropriately and carried either my resume or literature discretely in my bag in case someone asked to see it. I arrived at each meeting early, so I could mix with the parents, teachers, and principal over coffee. Then I would sit through some of the meeting. If I was lucky, the president of the PTA would introduce me as a special guest and allow me to say a few words. This was a perfect opportunity to get my message across about my belief in good public education. I also added that my own children went to public school and I had been a teacher. The biggest advantage of beginning my campaign early was that I was able to visit all of the schools before summer recess. By July, when all of the other candidates were just beginning their campaigns, schools were closed for the summer, and none of my opponents had the opportunity to attend any meetings. In September, before the general election, I went back to each school and was treated like an old friend. It gave me double exposure.

Not all of the schools were overwhelmingly friendly. When I arrived at one school, the PTA president told me I had a lot of nerve to think I could taint her meeting with a campaign appearance. She was about to dismiss me when another member of the PTA said, "Hold on. Do you realize that the State of Florida funds public education? This lady may someday be in a position to help us." What an enlightened woman! I will never forget the embarrassment she saved me. I couldn't have said it better myself. At another school, the president was friendly and supportive of my appearance, but the principal took one look at my campaign badge and walked away. At times like this, I needed nerves of steel. Many of the candidates in my area followed my lead and make a point of attending PTA meetings. Some schools even have a "Candidate Night" and invite the candidates who impact funding for public education to attend and speak. You will have a great advantage if you get to know the PTA members and their issues before the event. Politics is the art of making friends and getting to know many people. Next time you see a well-known politician in his or her district, see how many people he or she knows and how many people feel very comfortable with him or her. This comes from repeated visits to events instead of just a one-time appearance.

After each new PTA meeting, I would follow up by sending the president a thank-you note. Often it was added to the minutes of the meeting and sent to all the parents in a newsletter. The schools are very fertile ground for votes. Don't overlook them!

A final note worth mentioning: After the general election, I was lucky enough to have money left over in my campaign account. I divided the money equally among the PTAs and hand-delivered the checks at the large general meetings. As their state representative, I became a minor celebrity in the district.

- **Find out when PTA meetings are held.**

- **Attend as many PTA meetings as possible.**

- **Send a follow-up thank you to the president.**

- **Consider donating leftover campaign funds to schools.**

21

Campaigning in a Multicultural Community

E thnic communities have their own election-time traditions, and you would be wise to learn them if you hope to capture the vote there.

The Black Community

My district had a small but well-established African-American community in Coconut Grove, Florida. The area is historic and dates back to the 1800s, when people from the Bahamas first settled in Florida. It is now a mix of middle- and low-income citizens. Like all communities, it has well-connected leaders, and I made sure to find out who the leaders were. Over lunch one day, I told Mrs. Bentley, the president of the West Grove Homeowners'

Elect **Susan**
GUBER

STATE REPRESENTATIVE
DISTRICT 117
DEMOCRAT

Commissioner Barbara Carey
& Dr. Marvin Dunn Endorse Susan Guber
for Florida House Seat

"When our community is asked to choose between several candidates for a seat in the Florida House of Representatives, we look for someone who cares about the problems of working people, and who has the experience to get results in Tallahassee. That's why we are strongly supporting Susan Guber for the district that includes Coconut Grove, East Coral Gables, Key Biscayne and East Kendall. Susan has been very active in education all her adult life. She is deeply committed to improving the quality of schooling for our children. We hope you'll consider voting for Susan Guber for the Florida House of Representatives, District 117, on September 2nd."

Commissioner Barbara Carey
Dr. Marvin Dunn

Pd. Pol. Adv.   **PUNCH #111**

Oversized postcard targeted to ethnic community

Association, that I intended to run. She invited me to meet with her group. I went to several of the monthly meetings and became a common face there. By the end of the summer, I won the endorsement of the group. Mrs. Bentley herself even helped me in my door-to-door walks. She had been the school nurse in the area and she knew everyone. One of the African-American football players from the University of Miami said he would walk with me as well. Thus, I always managed to walk with a person from the community.

Traditionally, the black community encourages politicians to visit its churches. The churches serve the congregation as a community, educational, social, and religious center. This is different from many other religious facilities, where politics and politicians are ostracized. There were five churches in the area, and I was welcomed at each one and even given an opportunity to come to the pulpit to speak. I called the pastor ahead of time to let him know that I was coming. Again, by starting the campaign early, I was able to go to each church a couple of times during the campaign. People got to know me and feel comfortable with my candidacy.

Walking door to door and going to the churches was a good start, but the weekend before the election I really learned how to "get out the vote" in the black community. Palm cards that fit in the palm of your hand are distributed by leaders door to door. Each card has the slate of candidates written on it. The cards are also distributed at the polls the day of the election by a poll worker paid from your campaign funds. That person sits at the precinct with a sign from your campaign and hands out the cards. I also had one person bring the poll worker lunch so he would not have to leave the spot. In addition to delivering lunch, this man also rented a large van and gave rides to the polls. The African-American community has its own way of handling elections and it is best to find out what the customs are.

The Hispanic Community

Miami is now 51% Hispanic. The majority of Latin voters are Cuban Republicans. When I first ran, the Hispanic community comprised a small portion of the voting population in my district. Since it was not registered Democratic, I did not need to target these voters in the primary because they could not vote for me anyway. If this segment is in your party, you should send out literature in their native tongue and do the same for all your press messages. You should also try to make some speeches in

Spanish as well. Again, it is important to research the ways of the voters in the minority community.

The Jewish Community

Jewish people, many of them elderly, constitute a significant portion of my county. While the district I was running in did not contain many of the condominiums where they live, it is still interesting to note how campaigns are waged there. Because some of the condominiums are large enough to constitute their own precincts, there is a polling place in the lobby. In order to get out the vote in these huge complexes, you may need to hire someone to coordinate the condo campaign. This is usually a person who can encourage the condo leadership to support your candidacy. The coordinator assigns one or two people on each floor of the condo to get out the vote. The floor leaders knock on doors throughout election day, reminding residents to vote. They know who has voted by checking in with the person who monitors the polling station. At each residence, they hand out palm cards and ask the voters when they plan to vote that day. They even accompany the voter downstairs to the polls.

Some of the smaller condos are not large enough to constitute precincts and therefore do not have polling places in the lobby. Here, getting to the polls requires transportation. Volunteers with cars pick the voters up, hand out palm cards, and drive voters to the polls.

Your campaign staff condo coordinator will negotiate with the condo leaders to endorse your candidacy. As with any constituency, you will win some buildings and lose others. If you are well known and have been active and effective in the past, obviously your chances will be better than if you are new to the area. As mentioned earlier, many condos have a condo leader on the homeowners' association board who specializes in elections. He or she will be asked to host a breakfast for the candidate to meet the residents (the candidate pays for the breakfast). This is important because the leader is the master of ceremonies at the event and publicly demonstrates his or her support for your campaign. As the leader votes, so do most of the residents. The condo leader is supposed to know which candidate is best for the residents and is given much power in this regard. Again, by throwing your hat in the ring early on, you will be in a better position to hire the best and most influential condo coordinator.

As a result of the 1992 redistricting by the state legislatures, many of the minorities are now secluded in separate districts. In Florida, there are predominantly black or Hispanic districts. If you want to run in that area, it is almost impossible to win if you are not from that particular minority group. If, however, you have an area with an ethnic mix, by learning the mores of the community and doing your homework, you can win the ethnic vote!

- **Know the procedure for campaigning in each ethic community.**

- **Use a consultant in each community to guide you.**

- **Target mailings and advertising to appeal to minority communities.**

22

Creating the
Phone Bank

Getting the voters into your camp is quite an accomplishment. Getting them out to vote is quite another. For the latter, we used a "phone bank." About a week before the election, after we had finished our door-to-door campaign, we called everyone we had met to remind them to vote.

A friend who was in the insurance business had a large office with twenty phone lines. The office was near the district and was easy for volunteers to find. Any large office with lots of separate phone lines will do. We were fortunate to be able to use the office every night from seven to nine o'clock for one week prior to each election. This time slot worked out perfectly. The office was closed, and this was a great time to reach voters at home.

During the walking part of the campaign, my daughter would tell her volunteers about the phone bank, and people readily agreed to help. She spent the week prior to the phone bank calling all our volunteers, telling them about the phone bank schedule, and signing them up. Each evening during the week of the phone bank, the volunteers would gather outside the building and Elizabeth would bring them into the building. Because of nighttime security in the building, we were asked to bring everyone in at once. She then gave each volunteer a precinct list in alphabetical order. The lists included the names and phone numbers of the people we had visited on our walks. Also included were the notes we had made during the walks as well as our code letter. That was the advantage of walking. By going door to door and then looking up all the phone numbers of the people we had visited, we had all the ingredients for a fabulous phone bank. We were not cold calling. These people knew about our campaign, and we were now reminding them to vote. Elizabeth supplied each volunteer with a copy of my campaign literature and a short message to read. The literature included some notes about my background in case anyone asked. The phone message was very short and similar to the message used in canvassing. It read: "Hello, Mr. or Ms. (name on the list). I am calling from the Susan Guber campaign. Tuesday is Election Day. Please do not forget to vote." Our volunteers were careful not to use their own names when calling; we felt it would confuse the voters. We also did not ask anyone for their vote. We did not want to open the door for a negative response. We merely reminded people to go to the polls.

In the primary, with six Democratic candidates in the race, it was difficult for anyone to stand out from the pack. I must say, all my opponents were fine citizens, any one of whom would have been a decent legislator. However, our local newspaper, the *Miami Herald,* was a very powerful force in the district, and when I received the paper's glowing recommendation, I was ecstatic! This was a big break. It clearly distinguished my candidacy from the others, and I knew that people would take this recommendation into the voting booth. The night I won

The Miami Herald Recommends the Election of

SUSAN GUBER

To the Florida Legislature.

The Miami Herald said she has "...a sound grasp of the legislative process."

Susan Guber wants to get things done for Dade County! Here's why she can do the job others can't!

- Chairman, Citizens' Coalition for Public Schools
- Florida Bar Grievance Committee, Lay Representative
- Former Public School Teacher
- Coordinator, New World Festival of Arts
- Aide to State Rep. Betty Metcalf
- Chairman Dade County Common Cause
- Aide to County Commissioner Bill Oliver
- Member, Coral Gables, Kendall and Coconut Grove Chambers of Commerce

RECOMMENDED BY The **Miami News**

Best Qualified...BY FAR!
To hold down YOUR taxes. Improve YOUR quality of life. And Bring Back YOUR fair share from Tallahassee.

Elect Susan

GUBER

Florida House of Representatives

Thursday, September 25, 1986　w　The MIAMI HERALD

Pd Pol Adv　11

Newspaper advertisement

the paper's approval, I went to the phone bank, gathered all the volunteers into the common area, and told them the good news. My daughter added the following to the phone message: "Susan Guber has the *Miami Herald's* recommendation."

As the volunteers made their calls, they put a check mark next to each name called or marked NH if someone was not at home and there was no answering machine. We called the latter group the following night. We made a new list after each campaign, to get ready for the next election. We always kept our phone list updated. It took one week of phone-banking, with at least ten volunteers, to make all the calls throughout the district. The calls included only 60% of the registered voters, because 40% of them had unlisted numbers.

Rarely did we get a negative response, because we were dealing with people we had talked to on our walks. If we got one, we pulled that person's name from the list. Once in a while, we would pick up a volunteer from our phone calls. One woman we called asked, "Is Susie there?" When I got on the phone, she asked, "Where are you? I want to come over and help out." The next five nights, she and her husband came to work at the phone bank. That was an unexpected bonus.

I stayed at the phone bank as much as I could. Sometimes I had to go to a candidates' forum or give a speech, but I always tried to be there. Coming back from a rally, I would tiptoe into the office. It was always a thrill to see all the phones being used. It was important to me to take the time to thank each volunteer personally for coming. It was also important for me to stay on hand, since voters had questions about the issues that only I could answer. I always instructed volunteers not to answer these questions themselves. If I was not available, they were asked to jot down the phone number so I could call the person back.

Our phone bank was very well organized. It was an important component in the race and much easier to organize than anything else. Yet, if we hadn't canvassed door to door in the manner we did, it wouldn't have been nearly as effective.

- Calling all voters is the best way to get out the vote.

- Find a central location with multiple phone lines.

- Have your volunteer coordinator organize people to make phone calls.

- Prepare your phone message and have a copy for each volunteer.

- Keep a record of all phone calls completed.

23

Organizing the Poll Watchers

There are two categories of poll watchers. The one that is highly visible is the person who stands at the precinct the day of the election with a sign and passes out literature. In some ethnic communities, that visibility is important. In other more conservative precincts, it is considered bad taste. Know the mores in your area and what is considered appropriate for this category of poll watcher.

The other type of poll watcher is often overlooked but can make a difference in a tight race. A few months before the primary, I learned that in our county, a candidate can have a worker visit each polling place on election day and check to see who has voted. Of course, that person cannot see the actual finished ballot. When you vote, you are asked to sign in, and that sheet of paper becomes public record. It proves that you have exercised your right to vote and, of course, prevents you from voting twice. In order to take advantage of this information and find out if your "A" list voters have actually voted, you need a volunteer to take your phone bank list to the precinct and compare it with those who have actually been to the polls.

The law in my county requires that a certain form be filled out in triplicate in order to certify the poll watcher. Poll watchers must observe certain rules. For example, they can visit the polls only between the hours specified on the form, and they must never interfere with the voting process. They must wait until a time when it is relatively slow at the precinct to inspect the list. On primary election days, the turnout is usually very light, and it is easy to gain access to the list of people who have voted. Rather than have a poll watcher waste hours on end at one precinct, he or she can visit several precincts at intervals throughout the day to compare the voting lists with your list.

We had thirty-two precincts to cover, so I knew I would need many volunteers for this job. Also, they had to take time off on a work day. When I raised more money several elections later, I was able to pay temporary workers to do this job. As we identified volunteers in the first race, we had them fill out the proper forms. One copy was for the central elections office, one was for the precinct, and one was for our own files. The only rule for recruiting a poll watcher was that the person had to be a registered voter in the county. After all of the forms were filled out, we assembled kits for the poll watchers. Each kit included one copy of the form to give them access to the polls, the address of the polling place, and a list of people we had called during our phone bank. This format matched the alphabetical list that the precinct kept. At three o'clock in the afternoon on election day, each volunteer went to his or her assigned polling place. If it was quiet in the precinct, the poll worker read off the list of voters who had voted that day; if it was busy, the poll worker allowed

1. The pollwatcher cannot speak to any pollworker or elector--with the following exceptions:
   - to give their name and pollwatcher form to the precinct clerk upon entering the polling place.
   - to challenge an elector's right to vote with the clerk. *(The clerk will then inform the elector and complete the "Oath of Person Entering Challenge of Elector" form.*
   - they can speak with the clerk if they see or hear anything that does not comply with the law. *(The clerk is legally responsible and in charge of the election in the polling place. However, the pollwatcher can call the Elections Department at 375-5553 if they are not satisfied with the clerk's explanation or the handling of the situation--but cannot use the precinct phone.)*
2. The pollwatcher cannot bring any radios, television sets, or newspapers inside the polling place; cannot wear or display any political party, candidate or campaign materials.
3. The pollwatcher cannot interfere with the conduct of the election. They must sit or stand away from the voting equipment and ballot table; they cannot walk around the voting area.
4. The pollwatcher can inspect the precinct register only when the clerks are not processing electors. The inspectors are required to call out the names of electors loud enough for the pollwatchers to hear.
5. The pollwatcher can be in the polling place only during the times specified of the pollwatcher form. Anyone can be present to observe the opening and closing procedures as long as they do not interfere with the process.

Poll watcher information

1. Submit pollwatcher forms **no later than noon on the second Tuesday preceding the election** to the Supervisor of Elections in the Stephen P. Clark Center located at 111 NW 1 Street on the 19th floor. **These forms cannot be faxed!!**

2. If the candidate expects he or she will participate in more than one election for the office being sought, the pollwatcher coordinator can use the same form for <u>all</u> elections by listing <u>all</u> dates on the front of the form.

3. There is a limit of <u>one</u> precinct <u>per</u> form for <u>each</u> person acting as a pollwatcher. The forms are then given to the Elections Department in triplicate <u>and</u> in precinct numerical order. If the required amount of copies are not provided, there will be a 15 cents charge per page for copying costs.

4. Pollwatcher applications will be approved upon verification of the applicant's active status as a registered voter in Dade County. **Do not leave without obtaining the approved third copy-- this is given to the pollwatcher to obtain entrance to the polling place!**

5. All pollwatcher forms for <u>municipal</u> elections are returned to the respective City Clerk for processing **except for the cities of <u>Hialeah, Miami, and Miami Beach.</u>**

6. No candidate or law enforcement official can be designated as a pollwatcher.

Poll watcher application instructions

Precinct Number: _____   Hours: from _____ to _____
Núm. de Recinto: *Horario: de*   *a*

Pollwatcher is designated by the following candidate or political party:

_____

Election Dates: _____
Fechas de Elecciones:

                          _____

                          _____

The following individual, subject to the Elections Department verification of qualifications, is designated as a pollwatcher:

_____   _____
print name as it appears on registration card   registration number or date of birth
escriba con letra de imprenta los nombres y appelidos   *núm. de inscripción o fecha de nacimiento*
del modo que aparecen en la tarjeta de inscripción.

_____   _____
address   daytime telephone number
dirección   *núm. de teléfono por el dia*

                _____
                signature
                firma del observador electoral

Pollwatcher Coordinator: (print name) _____
Escriba con letra de imprenta nombres y appellidos del coordinador de observadores electorales.

Campaign office telephone number: _____
Núm. de teléfono de la campaña electoral:

                Metro - Date Elections Department
                111 NW 1 Street, Suite 1910
                Miami, Florida 33128
                (305) 375-5553

Poll watcher form

our poll watcher to check our list against the voting list. The poll watcher then called all of the people who had not yet voted and reminded them to get to the polls before they closed at seven in the evening.

Poll watching is a little used but effective technique for getting *your* voters out. When well organized, it can make the difference. On election day, I got on the phone myself to remind people to vote. Many times I would hear, "I'm so glad you called and reminded me. I almost forgot. Thanks for calling. By the way, what time do the polls close?" Don't leave anything to chance. Write people, call people, and even remind them over and over. You never know what gets people to the polls, so try everything.

- Find out if the elections department allows poll watchers.

- Have volunteers fill out the necessary forms.

- Call poll watchers to remind them of their duty.

- Have poll watchers pick up your list of voters the day before the election.

- Be on hand at headquarters and have backup volunteers in case you need extra help.

24

Dealing with Emotions

Running for office could have been emotionally and physically draining, but it was not. It was a very rewarding, exhilarating experience, and not just because I won. Two thoughts kept going through my mind during the year I was running. First, I had nothing to lose by becoming a candidate. Second, I began my campaign in earnest more than one year before the election and before anyone else in my race. If I lost, it wouldn't have been because I didn't try my best or didn't have enough time to do a thorough job.

Sometimes we set our sights on a project that puts our ego on the line. If things don't work out, we feel we failed and were unworthy. This could have easily happened. However, I viewed running as a test of new skills. In the beginning, I really did not believe I could win. I saw little chance of victory compared to several other possible candidates, who included a woman whose net worth was estimated to be in the millions, a physician/businessman who had advertisements for his insurance product on television, and an excellent former legislator. All of them were Democrats. I went in thinking, "We'll see how well I can do against all odds." With that in mind, I began running the best campaign I knew how. I felt as if I were in a horse race with blinders on and couldn't see what the others were doing. As it turned out, none of those potential candidates entered the race.

Perhaps by starting early, having my bus bench signs up six months before the election, and raising $54,000 in the same period of time, I discouraged more opposition. Many opponents filed their papers to run nine or ten months after I did. When they were just beginning to organize, I had already walked in seven precincts. Throughout the last months, I knew this and felt all the more confident. I also felt more secure when I saw our bumper stickers on ten cars a day and very few of the opponents'.

In *How to Win in Politics,* former Governor Fuller Warren of Florida writes of getting in shape for his campaign in the forties:

> From a long and hard experience in campaigning, extending over a period of twenty-two years (I ran my first race in 1926 as a candidate for the Legislature in Calhoun County) I recommend that a person planning to run for office get in the best physical condition possible. Smoking tobacco should be avoided, or at least done very sparingly. Smoking will cut a candidate's wind; wind, plenty of it, is indispensable in political campaigning.

That advice is not hard to argue with even today. He goes on to say:

> I recommend that a candidate lay off liquor. Whiskey won't mix successfully with campaigning. It will sap the energy and vitality that should go into satisfying the countless demands a campaign makes on a candidate's physical resources.
>
> I recommend deep breathing in the morning and at night—if you are not too tired, as I usually was. During my campaign for Governor, I began the day by walking

into an open place and inhaling, for a while, at least six deep breaths. Occasionally, when I had a spare minute or two, Jim Landon stopped the car on the road and I got out and took in two lungs full of fresh air and repeated the dose several times. You gotta (sic) take in the air if you are going to give out hot air!

I urge light calisthenics upon rising in the morning. You won't have enough energy at night; you will barely be able to untie your shoes.

I recommend a lot of orange juice and sweet milk for a candidate. Six glasses of orange juice and three glasses of milk a day are a minimum for a fast-running candidate; the use of less incurs risk of losing the race.

There is no substitute for sleep. Sleep not only "knits up the raveled sleeve of care", but does a lot of other things to the sleeper which are necessary to the winning of a political race. A candidate not in bed by 10:00 p.m. is flirting with defeat!

I had to laugh when I read this. But the routine worked for Governor Warren, and that's the important message.

I, too, had a routine and made sure that I didn't work against my "inner clock." I'm an early riser, and I enjoy an early jog or workout at the local gym. I also enjoy dinner with my family. These two activities are important to me both emotionally and physically. Throughout the campaign, I tried to follow my own rhythm. Some days I had several events to attend, but I knew it wouldn't hurt if I missed one or two. Walking door to door was the most important job, and it took precedence over everything else. It is best to prioritize and not fret about the rest. I attended breakfasts and luncheons but few dinners. I ate dinner with my family and was out the door ready to walk by around 6:30 p.m. Since it was light out in the summer, this schedule worked out well. On weekends, we would walk at 10:30 a.m. and again at 7:00 p.m.

The last days before the primary, I looked back and thought, "Win or lose, I've learned how to speak in public without fainting. I've learned how to raise money. I've learned how to sell myself. I now have a good grasp of current events. I've also brought my family together on a worthwhile project." I felt I had not wasted a year but rather gained some valuable new skills.

I might add that we did prevail. In a field of six primary candidates on the Democratic side, we took over 40% of the vote. After getting the most votes in this election, my confidence soared. It was great, but not good enough to avoid a runoff election. In Florida, if one primary candidate doesn't get more than 50% of the vote, then a runoff election is held. In the second primary, we took 62% of the vote and beat the other front-runner. In the general election, we squeaked by with 50.6% of the vote, which proved that all the work we had done was crucial. So begin early, pace yourself, and remember that you have nothing to lose. Who knows, you may even win!

- Begin your campaign and organization early in order to avoid extra stress.

- Focus on your own race and not your opponent's.

- Keep fit and in tune with your inner clock.

- Remember, win or lose, you're still a winner with the new skills, friends, and experiences you have acquired.

25

Handling Election Day

I t finally arrives—the day you have been looking forward to for so many months. You wake up in the morning and realize that that night you will either be a candidate again (if the race is a primary), an elected official (if it's a general general election), or out of business altogether (if you lose). There is little the candidate can do on election day except wait, and each hour seems endless.

After going through two difficult primary elections, Frank and I decided that we would have some fun on the day of the general election. Since my name is Guber, we bought little bags of "Goobers" candies and went from polling place to polling place, quietly leaving the candies with the poll watchers. I wore no badge; it wasn't allowed. Many of the poll watchers knew who I was; I thanked them all for their hard work and talked quietly to each one. We had thirty-two precincts, so it took most of the day to visit them all. Now, years later, when I see my former poll watchers, they remember the "Goobers."

At the end of the day, I came back to headquarters

Elect Susan GUBER

STATE REPRESENTATIVE
DISTRICT 117
DEMOCRAT

Dear Voter:

Sept. 2nd is a day of opportunity for Democratic voters in House District 117 -- an opportunity to select a qualified Democrat for the seat occupied by a Republican for the last 12 years. As my family and I have walked door-to-door, meeting you and other voters, we've learned first-hand about the important issues in this campaign -- improving our public schools, reducing crime, protecting our environment and halting overdevelopment. So please vote for Susan Guber on Sept. 2nd and put experience to work for you in Tallahassee.

PUNCH #111

Pd. Pol. Adv.

Oversized postcard sent to voters

(my home) and saw a dear friend working at the phones with Elizabeth. They were making last-minute calls to remind people to vote. Often I heard them say, "If I hadn't called, this lady wouldn't have voted." The most well-meaning people forget to vote, so every effort is necessary, right up to the last minute. We would leave messages on answering machines in case voters got home early enough to go back out to the polls to vote.

At around 5 p.m., the campaign volunteers and staff left. I took a nap, because I knew it was going to be a long night. Little did I know that it was going to be such a close race that we would not know for two days what the official final results were. At six o'clock, my husband and I went out for dinner. In the meantime, my volunteers were making preparations for the campaign party at a friend's house. Of course, I was much too anxious and excited to eat, but it was nice to do something normal and not campaign oriented for a change. When we came home, we watched the news until 8 p.m. and then got ready to go to what was to be our victory party.

- Make plans to keep busy during election day.
- Rest up for the long night ahead.
- Good luck!

26

Cleaning Up and Saying Thanks

Win or loose, the morning after election night is somewhat like a hangover. You are exhausted after months of campaigning, whether from the stress of the schedule or the battering by the press and opponents. Several thoughts came to my mind the morning after my first election. First was that I needed a vacation and some quiet time with my neglected family. A week would be ideal, but some officeholders must begin work the week after the election. Judges, legislators, school board members, and county commissioners must report to a training program in order to learn the process of their new office. Also, in many legislative bodies, a very political series of events for choosing leadership positions is held in the days following an election. In such instances, a vacation consists of little more than a long weekend. Taking time off at this point is like running in a marathon when all of a sudden the race stops. I found myself screeching emotionally to a halt, and it took me several days to wind down.

The next task was cleaning up the campaign office, closing it down, and making sure my signs were all removed throughout the district. In some communities, candidates with leftover campaign signs are fined. Many candidates keep campaign staff for a few days following a campaign to help with this process. For winners, the transition from campaign staff to legislative staff takes place at this time. The most loyal staff members are the people who worked for you in the campaign, but it is also wise to consider staff who know government and the process.

The last job is to thank voters and volunteers for their support. Some candidates put temporary stickers on their campaign signs saying a simple "thank you." I have even seen candidates standing out on a highway the day after an election with a big "thank-you" sign. It is a nice idea, and sometimes voters honk to show appreciation, but frankly I was too exhausted to even consider it. Some candidates put a small thank you in the local newspaper. If you have leftover campaign money, it is a very nice idea.

I always had either a luncheon or dinner for my volunteers. They are special people. Their work is unsung throughout the campaign, and they are invaluable. Before election day, I would budget for a party and leave a deposit with a restaurant or hotel for the occasion. I would choose a special menu and before dessert would make a short speech telling the volunteers how much I appreciated the work they did. I also asked each volunteer to stand and introduce himself or herself. Volunteering should be social, and I tried to make sure people got to know each other. I also had a favor for each volunteer to take home so that they wouldn't forget me. One year it was a plant, one year it was a clock that said "thanks for your time," and one year it was a jar of candy kisses with "kisses from Susie" inscribed on the jar Keeping volunteers happy and informed between elections is important for your next campaign.

It is important to maintain your image and character as an elected official. As a public figure, you will be judged by little details such as removing signs and thanking voters and volunteers. These jobs are as crucial as getting out the vote.

27

Conclusion

Running for office was the best learning experience I have ever had. I met a variety of people from many walks of life—from the lady in the wheelchair whose home I walked to (who had heard about me before and was anxious to meet me) to the children in the Fourth of July parade on Key Biscayne. They all bring back wonderful memories. The fourteen-month campaign gave my family and me an opportunity to work on a project as a team, although there were days when my husband walked door to door in the pouring rain, when my daughter called for volunteers and everyone turned her down, and when I was at a speaking engagement until midnight and came home exhausted. My eldest daughter, Carolyn, came home from law school in New York City one weekend and spent the whole time canvassing.

Behind the whole episode was the knowledge that this was a very unscientific, unpredictable process. No matter how one prepares, one can lose. But I knew that however the election turned out, I had given it a good try and had grown through the experience. The night of the

general election, November 4, was my forty-eighth birthday. Good friends hosted the election-night party. Their
home is lovely and large. Volunteers had the food and
drinks ready, complete with a surprise birthday cake. My
husband and I arrived to a full house of well-wishers
waiting for the election results. We had been to many of
our friends' festive and beautiful parties, but this one
included little lights in the trees, candles, tables with long
floral tablecloths, a bar, music, and balloons. As I looked
around, I saw it was truly special and a tribute to the
fourteen long months we had all given to the campaign.
We watched the results on television. We even had a
friend down at election central call us on a private phone
number with the results before they were broadcast. We
were ahead early in the evening, but as the night wore
on, the margin became narrower. I managed to maintain
the lead, but the race was so close that it would be two
days before we could claim a legal victory. (The absentee
ballots take two days after an election to verify.)

Late on the night of the election, for the first time—
after all the writing and practicing of the speeches, stuffing the envelopes, planning the schedules, calling for
money, walking to houses, and pacing the floor at all
hours of the morning—I felt like all the hard work had
paid off. I was a winner. I had also won a personal victory
in following through on such an enormous project. (Years
later, I met a state representative and casually asked how
many constituents he had in his district. He said he had
7,000. I then realized how big Florida's districts are. When
I ran, I had 85,000 constituents. I also realized what an
enormous undertaking it was to walk the whole district!)
Taking chances and working to the maximum had been
exhilarating for me. Yet all too often, one hears of candidates who ruin their home life and deplete their financial
and emotional resources. That needn't be the case. Campaigning can be a family project, with positive results for
everyone, regardless of the outcome. We won and gained
in the process, and you can, too.

By two o'clock in the morning, as I sat in front of the television set with my family and close friends, my husband and daughter put their arms around me and said, "We're so proud of you, Representative Guber." Tears welled up in my eyes. It had been a long year, a long day, and a very long evening. But for me, there was nothing more gratifying than the knowledge that I had won, through hard work, a hard-fought political campaign.

- **Campaigning for election can be the experience of a lifetime. When it is finally over, relax and enjoy it!**